Quick Learning Kits

Math & Science

Written by
Linda Milliken

Contributing editor
Ellen Sussman

Illustrated by
Barb Lorseyedi

Contributing artist
Andrea Tarman

© 1992 **EDUPRESS**   • PO Box 883   • Dana Point, CA 92629

ISBN 1-56472-006-3

TABLE OF CONTENTS
Math

TABLE OF CONTENTS
Science

Teaching Notes

These easy-to-assemble kits will provide students of all ages with hours of learning across the curriculum. There are several ways the kits can be incorporated in classroom learning. The option you select should suit your philosophy and needs. You may want to implement the kits in several ways.

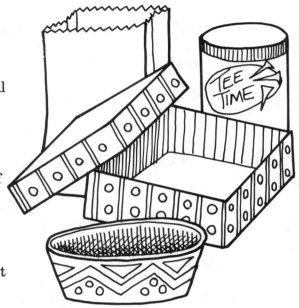

CENTERS:
- Introduce kits in a center based on literature or curriculum themes currently being studied in your classroom.
- Develop a center designed to feature a variety of kits for children to explore and enjoy according to personal choice. Introduce new kits throughout the year to maintain interest level. Announce the addition of a new kit with fanfare and explanation!

INDEPENDENT LEARNING:
- Have the kits available for use during specific blocks of time or spare classroom moments.
- Set aside conference time for students to ask questions and discuss their findings with you, a trained aide or parent volunteer.
- Number each kit and provide a check-out list that enables students to take the kits home for enrichment and parent involvement.

COOPERATIVE LEARNING:
- Complete projects as a group, then encourage students to try the activity again.
- Plan time for students to share their favorite kits and discoveries with classmates.
- Suggest MORE TO EXPLORE projects for individuals or small groups to pursue on their own.

CONTENT DESCRIPTION:
Each kit is presented in a two-page format.

The first page is a teacher's guide. It provides:
- *Summary*—a brief look at the kit's focus
- *Skills*—summary of skill objectives
- *Materials*—what is needed for kit assembly
- *Preparation*—complete instructions for kit assembly
- *Literature Links*—related reading to share together or independently
- *Writing Sparks*—related writing activities and topics
- *More to Explore*—related projects for further learning and exploration

Incorporate related learning suggestions—*literature links, writing sparks, more to explore*—
- as extensions of kit discoveries
- to spark interest in a theme or subject
- as introduction to a kit

The second page is for kit development. It provides:
- Kit cover
- Student Directions
- Inventory Checklist
- Things to Think About—student thought provokers

Kit Preparation

ASSEMBLY DIRECTIONS:
- Assemble all necessary materials.
- Follow instructions for any additional needs or patterns.
- Select a container appropriate in size and shape for the contents. (See KIT TIPS below.) In some instances, a specific container is required. That information is noted in the preparation instructions.
- Cover the container, if necessary, with giftwrap, construction paper or fabric.
- Reproduce the kit development page.
    There are two parts:
    Cover—Color, cut out, and glue the cover to the kit container. The more visually appealing the cover, the more students will want to explore the contents. Use a variety of medium—markers, crayons, colored pencils, watercolors. Feel free to add trims that coordinate with the kit's theme. Look for KIT TIPS in the preparation section for ideas.
    Contents—Trim the Student Directions, Inventory Checklist and Things To Think About to fit. Glue them in an easily readable place inside or outside the kit.

KIT TIPS
- Don't overlook any possibility as a container for your kits. The more variety the more interesting the kits will be for your students. Recycle shoe, cigar and gift boxes. Clean out coffee tins, nut cans and margarine tubs. Check garage sales for unusual bins, tins and boxes. Even a large zip top bag makes a nifty container.
- Laminating kit title, patterns and student directions will extend the life of the kit. Clear contact paper also works well.
- Make a list of "needed" materials to duplicate and send home to parents. Their contributions will make it easy and inexpensive to assemble the kits. Make a list of literature links that parents can purchase and give as gifts to the classroom or for a child's birthday—instead of cupcakes! Include a bookplate with the student's name.

TIME SAVERS
- Show parents how to assemble the kits. Ask each one to contribute materials and / or construction of one kit. Invite older students or a youth group looking for a service project to help with construction.
- Some kit materials are consumable. Design a "kit material" form for students to complete for any for any kits that need restocking. Decorate a coffee can for your desk. Ask students to drop the forms in the coffee can. Assign a "kit monitor" to check the forms and restock the kits.
- Number each kit so that tracking kit inventory will be easier. Keep a master sheet of kit title and corresponding number.
- Ask students and parents to submit their own ideas for kits. Offer extra credit for developing and demonstrating a learning kit to the class. Add it to your classroom collection.

Preparing the students
- Explain Learning Kit procedures
- Discuss inventory checklist
- Review check-out procedure and return
- Discuss kit care

Pick a Pattern

Simple geometric shapes provide a fun challenge as students try to create simple—and complicated—patterns.

SKILLS

- shape recognition • sorting
- recognizing patterns, repetition
- visual memory
- small motor

PREPARATION

Materials:

- 2 shoelaces (bright color)
- 4-6 colors poster board
- zip top bags • scissors
- shape patterns, page 92.

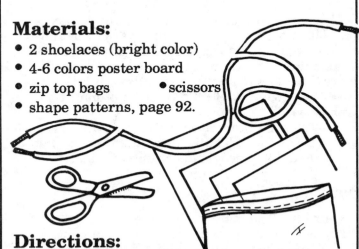

Directions:

1. Assemble all materials. Prepare the kit container and cover according to directions on page 5.
2. Trace four to six geometric patterns on the poster board. Cut at least 8 of each shape per color. Shape patterns are found on page 92.
3. Sort the shapes into individual zip top bags.

LITERATURE LINKS

Patterns and Puzzles in Mathematics; *Sylvia Horne.* Recreates patterns found in math.

Patterns Of Nature Photos; *Jeffrey Baker.* Helps students identify patterns in their natural surroundings.

Jump, Frog, Jump; *Robert Kalan.* An example of repetition and use of pattern in literature.

WRITING SPARKS

- Create *related-word* patterns. Illustrate them.
  For example:
  monkey, banana • monkey, banana
  beach, shell, waves • beach, shell, waves
- Write a story in which a phrase, sentence, or group of words is repeated. (See **LINKS**)
- Cut and paste picture patterns.

MORE TO EXPLORE

✔ Use graph paper to create color patterns. Vary the size of the grid to suit the age level of the students.

✔ Repetition is an important principle of design and patterns. Work in groups to look through wallpaper books and fabric swatches to identify patterns. Share group findings with classmates. Ask each group to design wallpaper.

✔ Discover patterns in areas such as literature and nature.

✔ Have a **Pattern for the Day.** Hang a length of clothesline. Provide clothespins and construction paper shapes. Change the pattern each morning. Begin the day by asking students to identify the pattern. Invite students to create the pattern for the day.

✔ Test listening skills. Say patterns out loud. Ask students to repeat them.

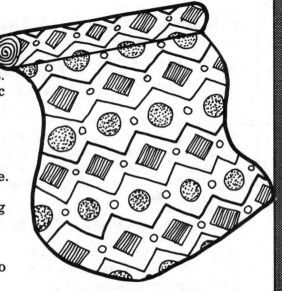

Pick-a-Pattern

-------------------------- Cut and tape student directions inside kit. --------------------------

DIRECTIONS
Pick a partner and create patterns.

1. Take the shapes out of their bags and keep them in neat piles in front of you.

2. Use the shapes to make **patterns.** <u>For example:</u>
circle, square•circle, square•circle, square   oval, square, square•oval, square, square

○ ☐ ○ ☐ ○ ☐   ⬭ ☐ ☐ ⬭ ☐ ☐

These are both simple patterns. Do you see how they repeat? (Look at the • between the words.
That is the spot that the pattern starts again.)

3. Lay the shapes on the table in front of you. Check the pattern. Whan you are sure the shapes are
in order, string them on the shoelace. Give the lace to a partner and ask him or her to figure out
the pattern. The partner will say the pattern out loud. Tell him or her if they are right or if they
need to try again. Making some easy and some hard. Can you use color in the pattern, too?

Inventory Checklist

☐ 2 shoelaces   ☐ shapes

- Sort all the shapes and put them back in
  their bags. The circles go in one, the
  triangles in another, and so on.
- Be sure the shoelace is not tangled or
  knotted when you return it to the kit.

Things to Think About

- Which patterns did you or your partner have
  trouble figuring out?

- What was the hardest pattern you made? How
  many shapes did it have? Did it have color?

- What patterns do you see around you? Look at the
  material in your clothing. Look at the print in
  the carpeting or flooring of your classroom.

No-Bore Boards

> *Students won't be bored when they use these easy-to-make geo-boards to reinforce shape recognition and develop visual skills.*

SKILLS

- shape recognition
- size comparison
- eye-hand coordination
- vocabulary development

PREPARATION

Materials:

- FOR GEO-BOARD:
  - 25 - 1" (2.54 cm) nails
  - 6" (15.25 cm) square block of wood (1"-2" or 2.5-5 cm) thick
  - sandpaper • hammer

- FOR STUDENT KIT:
  - geo-board • shape cards, pages 94-95
  - rubber bands...assorted colors & widths

Directions:

1. Assemble all materials. Prepare the kit container and cover according to directions on page 5.
2. **To make the geo-board:**
   - Sand the wood to smooth the edges.
   - Hammer the nails at 1" (2.54 cm) intervals. Leave 1" (2.54 cm) border on all sides. (See diagram)
3. Cut apart and laminate shape cards, pages 94-95.

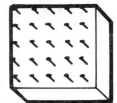

LITERATURE LINKS

Listen to a Shape; Marcia Brown. A variety of shapes are explored in simple text and colred photographs.

Math Fun with Tricky Lines and Shapes; Rose Wyler & Mary Elting. Older students will build a geometric vocabulary and enjoy the brain teasers as they look at different lines and shapes.

Boxes! Boxes!; Leonard Everett Fisher. An introduction to boxes of all sizes and shapes.

WRITING SPARKS

- Develop a shape book. Include vocabulary, written descriptions and magazine graphics.

- You are on the roof of your house looking down. Diagram the floorplan shapes you see.

- Use shape expressions as story starters...
  - *... He's such a square ... She's well-rounded*
  - *... There were many sides to the story*
  - *... Here's a new angle*

MORE TO EXPLORE

✔ Exercise, plant flowers and create shapes ... all at the same time! Find a location that needs beautification. Use shovels or trowels to dig holes in a specified shape. Plant seeds, plants or flowers donated by parents.

✔ Create a human geo-board. Stand in a grid formation. Pass a yarn ball from child to child to make geometric shapes.

✔ Draw multi-sided shapes with the same number of sides. Compare results. How many different shapes were created? Are any two the same?

✔ Build a geometric vocabulary. Incorporate *octagon, hexagon, quadrilateral,* etc. into classroom discussions and instructions. "Please put your chairs in the shape of a pentagon for reading time."

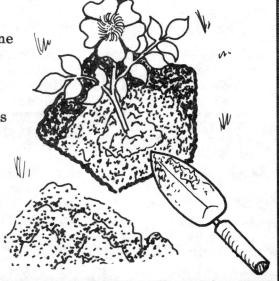

Color, cut and laminate for kit cover.
See preparation instructions, page 5.

Reproduce Page for Use in Student Kit

-- Cut and tape student directions inside kit. --

DIRECTIONS

1. Practice hooking a rubberband around the nails to make a shape. Move the rubberband to make the shape bigger, then smaller. When you can do this, go on to step 2.

2. Choose a shape card. Look at it carefully. Use a rubberband to make the same shape on the geo-board. Try to make the size and angles the same.

3. Try some shapes on your own. Make a ...
- pentagon — 5 sides
- hexagon — 6 sides
- octagon — 8 sides
- polygon — many sides

4. Create a shape with **dimension**. Put several rubberbands on the geo-board. Put the first one ow on the nails, the next one a little higher and so on. Start with a triangle, add a square, top it with a hexagon—or any combination of shapes you want. Make several.

Inventory Checklist

❑ rubberbands   ❑ geo-board
❑ shape cards

- Return all rubberbands to the bag. Make sure you haven't left any on the board.

- Count the shape cards. There are 12.

Things to Think About

- Look **down** at the shape you made with several rubberbands. How many shapes were created where the bands overlapped? Could you draw what you see? Try it!

- How many different kinds of 5-sided shapes could you make? 6-sided? 8-sided?

- How many tries did it take to match your geo-board shape to the one on the shape card?

Memory Shape-up

It may be easy to recognize shapes, but remembering their size as you see them in every day life is more difficult.

SKILLS

- shape recognition
- size discrimination
- visual memory
- application

PREPARATION

Materials:

- stick of chewing gum
- standard playing card
- cocktail napkin
- #1 coffee filter (triangular)
- plastic tab from loaf of bread
- paper
- plastic egg
- poker chip
- button
- small ruler

Directions:

1. Assemble all materials. Prepare the kit container and cover according to directions on page 5.

LITERATURE LINKS

Everything Has a Shape and Everything Has a Size; Bernice Kohn. An introduction to the shapes and sizes of everyday things.

The Wing on a Flea: A Book About Shapes; Ed Emberley. How to identify shapes in everyday objects ... through rhymes.

Amazing Look Through Book; Ed Emberley. Identify shapes through puzzles.

WRITING SPARKS

- Divide paper into columns. Head each with a shape. Brainstorm lists of everyday objects that fit under each heading.

- If I were a shape I would be a ...

- Describe your favorite dessert shape. Try ...
  - circle—scoop of chocolate ice cream
  - triangle—piece of lemon pie
  - square—brownie

MORE TO EXPLORE

- Guess the length of objects in feet and inches, then in metric equivalent. Measure actual size.

- Look around the room and identify the shape of everyday things. Take a walk outside and do the same. Which shape do you see the most?

- Have a debate ... which shape is the most useful in daily life?

- Bake (or bring in) a variety of cookies. Make a chart showing the variety of shapes.

- Shape up at lunch time. Eat together and examine the shape of things in your lunch.

Color, cut and laminate for kit cover.
See preparation instructions, page 5.

Reproduce Page for Use in Student Kit

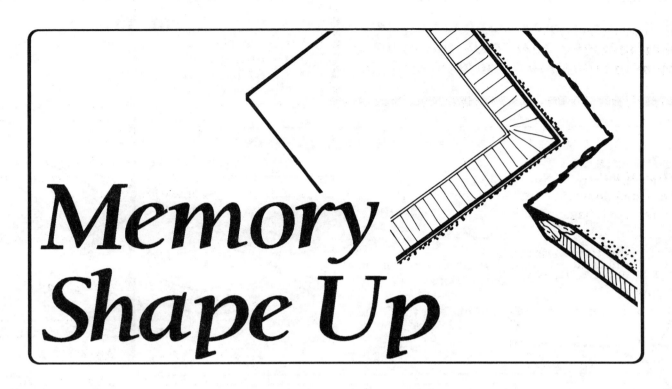

Memory Shape Up

-------------------------------------- Cut and tape student directions inside kit. --------------------------------------

DIRECTIONS

1. Take the objects out of the kit and study the size of each.
Pick them up and feel them. Turn them over in your hands.

2. Choose one to put back in the kit—or out of sight.
Draw the outline of that object on your paper.
Try to remember its exact size. Take the object out again .
Set it **on** the outline you drew. How close were you?

3. Repeat this with everything in the kit.

You can try this as many times as you want. Did you improve?

Inventory Checklist

☐ stick of chewing gum   ☐ plastic egg
☐ standard playing card ☐ poker chip
☐ napkin   ☐ button
☐ coffee filter   ☐ small rule
☐ plastic tab from loaf of bread
☐ paper
• Add more paper if needed.

Things to Think About

• Did it help to feel everything before you tried to draw them?

• Was there a shape or size easier for you to match?

• How close to the actual size of each object were you able to remember and draw? Measure the differences.

Count and Estimate

Simple "kitchen cupboard" items provide lots of insight into understanding numerical value.

SKILLS
- counting
- numerical value
- size/space relationships
- estimating

PREPARATION

Materials:
- dried kidney beans, white beans, peas
- 4 jar lids
- 3 zip-top bags

Directions:
1. Assemble all materials. Prepare the kit container and cover according to directions on page 5.

2. Spray paint each lid a bright color (optional).

3. Sort the dried beans and store in individual ziptop poly bags.

LITERATURE LINKS

Billions of Bugs: *Haris Petie.* Intriguing counting for all ages. Pages swarm with bugs, from one praying mantis to 1000 butterflies.

How Much is a Million?: *David Schwartz.* A million, a billion, a trillion . . . Introduces estimating large numbers and their relativity.

Weird Wonders and Bizarre Blunders: *Brad Schreiber.* A collection of funny, fictitious world records. Provides new ways to look at numbers!

MORE TO EXPLORE

✔ Experiment with other objects such as buttons or stones to increase understanding of size/space relationships.

✔ Work in reverse. Fill a lid. Try to estimate how many objects it holds. Count to see how close your estimate was.

✔ Start a "number collection". Choose an item to collect—bottle caps, pop-top tabs , buttons, etc. Then choose a large number—300 for example—and save the item in a large jar or bag. How much space do 300 pop top tabs occupy? Compare results with other collections.

✔ Students can sponsor an estimating contest. Fill a jar, box or bag with marbles or jelly beans. Ask other classes or classmates to write their estimate on an entry form. Check the entries and declare a winner.

✔ Look through the Guiness Book of World Records for "the most"— for example, the most people in a telephone booth. Talk about your findings.

Color, cut and laminate for kit cover.
See preparation instructions, page 5.

Reproduce Page for Use in Student Kit

Count and Estimate

-- Cut and tape student directions inside kit --

Directions

1. Get a piece of paper and pencil. Set the lids in front of you. Try to guess how many red beans will fit into the first lid. Write your estimate on the paper. Fill the lid, one bean at a time, counting each one you put in the lid.

2. Try to write a problem that will help you figure out the difference between your estimate and the actual number of items that fit into the lid.

3. Repeat the steps with the rest of the lids.

4. Repeat the steps with the rest of the beans.

Inventory Checklist

☐ 4 lids

☐ 3 bags of beans

• Be sure the beans and peas are sorted and that each bag contains only one kind.

• Seal the bags tightly.

Things to think about

• Did the size or shape of the lid make a difference in the number of beans it would hold?

• Did the size or shape of the bean or pea make a difference in the how many the lid held? How close were your estimates?

• In what ways could estimating help you in your life?

13

EVEN IF IT'S ODD

This puzzler provides an opportunity for problem solving using even and odd numbers.

SKILLS

- problem solving
- even/odd numbers
- application
- association

PREPARATION

Materials:
- three plastic cups
- eleven paper clips

Directions:
1. Assemble all materials. Prepare the kit container and cover according to directions on page 5.

LITERATURE LINKS

The Doorbell Rang; *Pat Hutchins.* Each ring of the doorbell brings more friends to share a dozen cookies. How will they be divided evenly?

Counting; Odd One Out; *John Satchwell.* A beginning concept book.

Dancing In the Moon; Counting Rhymes; *Fritz Eichenberg.* Illustrated verses from 1-20. Read the even ones on even calendar dates, the odd numbers on odd calendar dates.

WRITING SPARKS

ℓ Finish these oddities with an answer and a description ...
- The oddest animal I've ever seen is ...
- The oddest meal I've ever eaten is ...
- The oddest thing I've ever done is...

ℓ Would you rather play in a group of two or three? Why?

ℓ What does it mean to be *even-tempered*?

MORE TO EXPLORE

✔ Have counting contests. Who can count the fastest by twos? by odd numbers? by tens? by fives?

✔ Clean up by the numbers. One day pick up an even number of items off the floor. The next day pick up an odd number.

✔ Plan classroom activities by calendar dates. For example, on even numbered days, have silent reading time. On odd numbered days, have oral reading time.

✔ Study sports scores. Are the points scored even or odd? For example, a field goal in basketball is worth an even number of points unless, of course, it's from behind the three point line and then it's an odd number score! Make a list of sports and scores.

✔ Divide into groups of even and odd numbered students for cooperative learning activities.

Color, cut and laminate for kit cover.
See preparation instructions, page 5.

Reproduce Page for Use in Student Kit

-- Cut and tape student directions inside kit. --

DIRECTIONS
Remember these number rules:
Even numbers are 2, 4, 6, 8, 10 and so on.
Odd numbers are 1, 3, 5, 7, 9 and so on.

1. Line the three cups in a row.

2. Try to put the 11 paper clips into the cups so that there are an odd number of objects in each cup Keep trying until you are successful. It can be done. There must be at least one clip in each cup.

3. Now, put on your thinking cap and see how many different ways you can do it.

4. Get rid of one of the cups. Now there are 2 cups (an even number). Try again to have an **odd** number of clips in each cup. It's not as easy as you think!

Inventory Checklist

☐ 3 cups
☐ 11 paper clips

• Count each item to be sure you are putting the right number back into the kit.

Things to Think About

• Which puzzle was easier to figure out?

• No matter how high you count, what numbers do even numbers always end in? What about odd numbers?

• Why are the numbers called even or odd? What happens when you try to share an odd number of things?

TEE TIME

Predicting answers based on a collection of data is an important mathematical skill and one you can introduce with this activity.

SKILLS

- predicting
- collecting data
- drawing conclusions
- counting

PREPARATION

Materials:

- 3 paper plates—small, medium and large
- 25 golf tees in a variety of colors
- zip top bag (for storing tees)

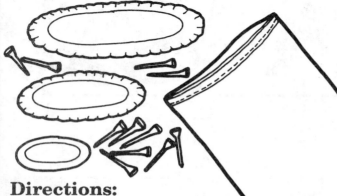

Directions:

1. Assemble all materials. Prepare the kit container and cover according to directions on page 5.

2. Put the tees in a zip top bag.

LITERATURE LINKS

The Dog That Called the Signals; *Matt Christopher.* One in a series of books about a telepathic dog, his pal, and their silly success in sports!

Fortune Telling; *Margaret Baldwin.* Discusses "fortune telling" and predicting through the use of crystal balls and palm reading.

In the Future; *Gail Stewart.* Excitng new technology for the future.

WRITING SPARKS

- Make five predictions for the school year. Seal them in an envelope. Open the envelope during the last week of school. How many predictions were accurate?

- Pretend you are a fortune teller. Choose a famous person and predict his or her future.

- Predict YOUR future. What will you be doing 10 years from now? 30 years? 50 years?

MORE TO EXPLORE

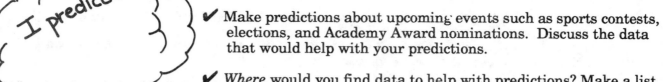

✔ Make predictions about upcoming events such as sports contests, elections, and Academy Award nominations. Discuss the data that would help with your predictions.

✔ *Where* would you find data to help with predictions? Make a list of the possible resources.

✔ Predict the weather for the upcoming week. How accurate were you? How could you have improved your predictions?

✔ Cut out current events that involve predicting the outcome of events. Highlight the data that helped determine the prediction.

✔ Can we really predict the future? Find out about *astrology* and *fortune telling*. What is *telepathy? ESP?* Give your opinion.

Color, cut and laminate for kit cover.
See preparation instructions, page 5.

Reproduce Page for Use in Student Kit

TEE TIME

-------------------------------- Cut and tape student directions inside kit. --------------------------------

DIRECTIONS

1. Put the three plates in a row on the floor in front of you. Stand next to the plates. Hold a tee in your hand. Reach out your arm, waist level, and drop the tee on the largest plate. Continue this with all the tees. Count how many stayed on the plate. Write down the results. Pick up all the tees and repeat this with the other plates. Keep track of the results.

2. Now change the experiment. With each change, try to predict the number of golf tees that will land and and **stay** on the plates. Here are some different ways to try:

- Put the plates on a carpeted floor. Then put them on a tile floor.
- Change the way you are holding the tee when you drop it.
- Drop the tees from different heights.

Inventory Checklist

☐ 25 golf tees ☐ 3 paper plates

- Checked the floor for tees. Some may have bounced. Check around **and** under the furniture. Put them in the bag.

- Stack the plates by size before putting them back in the kit.

Things to Think About

- Try to use the data (results) from the first experiment o help you predict the results of the other attempts.

- How did the size of the circle, the height at which the tee was dropped and the surface the plates were on affect the number of tees that landed on the plates?

PIZZA PARTY

A favorite meal becomes an appetizing lesson in mathematical skills, and an introduction to probability.

SKILLS

- calculating combinations
- sorting
- introduction to probability

PREPARATION

Materials:

- construction paper in a variety of colors—red, tan, black, green, brown
- 10 snack-size paper plate (pizza crusts)
- pizza ingredient patterns, page 92

Directions:

1. Assemble all materials. Prepare the kit and cover according to directions on page 5.
2. Use the patterns, page 92, to cut pizza "ingredients" from construction paper—black olives, red pepperoni, green bell pepper, brown mushrooms. (Include more for older students.) Store them separately in zip

LITERATURE LINKS

Fast-Food Guide; *Jacobson and Fritschner.* Reveals nutritional value of items at fast-food chains.

Good For Me; *Marilyn Burns.* Origins of a variety of foods are explored.

How Pizza Came to Queens; *Dayal Kaur Khalsa.* Charming story of a thoughtful girl helping an Italian visitor to her city.

WRITING SPARKS

⧸ Describe your favorite pizza ingredients.

⧸ Plan a Pizza Party. Decide on a theme. Plan decorations, games and refreshments (to have with your pizza, of course). Design invitations.

⧸ Create imaginative pizzas. For example, a monkey might enjoy a banana pizza. A golfer might want golf balls and tees.

MORE TO EXPLORE

✔ Plan a class **Pizza Party** (See WRITING SPARKS) Discuss the different pizza combinations you could order. How hard is it to agree on a selection of ingredients?

✔ Graph **PIZZA PREFERENCES.** Determine which ingredients are the *most popular* among classmates ... *least popular.*

✔ Visit a Pizza Parlor. Learn how pizzas are made. Compare nutritional value to other fast food fare.

✔ Research the origin of Pizza (See LITERATURE LINKS.) In committees, research other food origins.

✔ Find out which ingredients are the most nutritious.

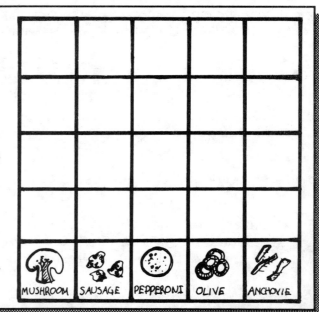

Color, cut and laminate for kit cover. See preparation instructions, page 5.

-------- Cut and tape student directions inside kit. --------

DIRECTIONS

1. Separate the paper plates (pizza crusts) and spread them out on the desk in front of you.

2. Take out all the ingredients from the bags but keep them in separate piles.

3. Prepare pizzas by putting ingredients on each crust. How many different combinations of pizza do you think you can make? Write your estimate on a piece of paper. Remember, each pizza must be different. You can use the same ingredients on some but at least **one** ingredient must be different. If you run out of crusts , just put your ingredients in piles, or get more plates.

Here are some possibilities: cheese, mushrooms, olives
cheese, pepperoni, olives
cheese, pepperoni, mushrooms

Get the idea?
That's three ... and that's just the beginning. **GET COOKING!**

Inventory Checklist

❏ Restack the plates carefully.

❏ Sort the ingredients and put them back into the zip top bags.

Things to think about

• How many different combinations did you create? How close was your estimate?

• How could you have figured out the number of combinations mathematically?

• The next time you are in a pizza parlor, look at the list of ingredients. How many different combinations would it be possible to make? Ask the cooks if they know the answer.

Everything In Its Place

Here's a hands-on activity that will make understanding place value a visual experience!

SKILLS

- application
- reading numerals
- visualizing quantity
- greater than, less than

PREPARATION

Materials:

- chinese jacks—small plastic rings available in the toy section of supermarkets, variety and party shops. If jacks can't be found, laminate paper circles with a hole in the center.
- Place value number cards, pages 94-95
- 6 nails   • hammer   • sandpaper
- piece of wood 3" (7.5 cm) x12" (30 cm)

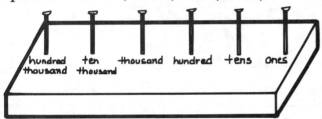

hundred thousand | ten thousand | thousand | hundred | tens | ones

Directions:

1. Assemble all materials. Prepare the kit container according to directions on page 5.
2. Sand the wood. Hammer the nails at 2" (5cm) intervals. Use permanent marker to Label each nail with a place value. See illustration.

LITERATURE LINKS

17 Kings and 42 Elephants; *Steven Kellogg.* Glowing paintings enhance this tale of a royal procession through a jungle paradise.

Teddy Bears' MovingDay; *Susanna Gretz.* Faced with changing houses, organization is difficult especially for one bumbling bear who can't keep anything in its place.

How Much is a Million?; *David Schwartz.* Shows concept of really big numbers.

WRITING SPARKS

✐ Make up an object to go with the number 12,362. Use it as a story starter ...
- 12,362 bugs were in my lunch today!
- Mom cooked 12,362 pancakes this morning!

✐ Make some numerical decisions. Which would you rather have ...
... 16 presents or 2 good friends?
... 5 chocolate cookies or 25 jelly beans?

MORE TO EXPLORE

✔ Pile up some place values. Use stones, marbles, beans or any other object to count and make a visual picture of place value. Increase the understanding that a two in the tens column actually means 20.

✔ Write numbers on poster board. Give each child a number card to hold. Call out names. As names are called, students come to the front of the class and stand in a row. Ask a student still seated to read the number that has been created.

✔ Play a variation of the game above. Divide into groups. Give each member a number card with a valuefrom 0-9. Call out numbers based on the cards. Students in each group arrange themselves in a row to reflect the number.

Color, cut and laminate for kit cover.
See preparation instructions, page 5.

Reproduce Page for Use in Student Kit

Everything In Its Place

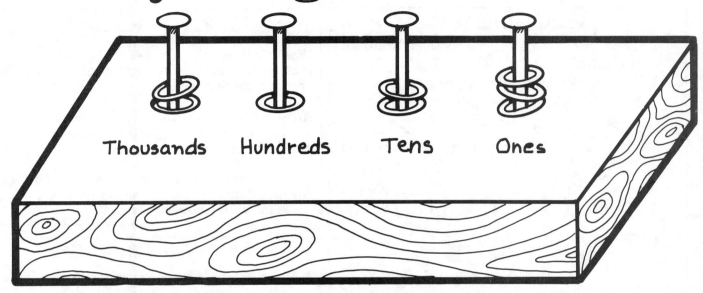

Thousands   Hundreds   Tens   Ones

-------- Cut and tape student directions inside kit. --------

DIRECTIONS

1. Choose a number card. Look at the number on the right. This number is in the <u>ones column.</u>

2. Put the same number of jacks on the nail above the word that says **ONES**.

3. Now look one number to the left. Put this number of jacks on the nail over **TENS.**

4. Keep reading one number to the left and putting the jacks on the board.
   (Look at the kit cover for help if you do not understand.)

5. Say the number out loud. When you have finished a card, take off the jacks and start over with a new card.

Inventory Checklist

☐ 24 number cards
☐ Chinese jacks (or rings)

• Count the number cards to be sure you return 24 to the kit.
• Put all the rings back into the bag and close the bag tightly.

Things to Think About

• Look at the place value names on the board. If the board were longer, what would the places added on the left would be called? Is there a pattern?

• Try to picture piles of things in your mind as you put the jack in its place on the board. If you are in the tens column, each jack means there is a pile of ten things. So two jacks means 20. What would 6 jacks mean?

21

Rope a Problem

Toss the dice. Where it lands, nobody knows. What we do know is that this will make math much more fun—at any ability level!

SKILLS

- computational skills
- writing mathematical sentences
- greater than, less than
- set identification

PREPARATION

Materials:
- two 2-foot (60 cm) lengths of yarn
- 6 die

Directions:
1. Assemble all materials. Prepare the kit container and cover according to directions on page 5.
2. Store the dice in a small bag.
3. Dip the ends of the yarn in wax or hot glue so the strands will not unravel.

LITERATURE LINKS

World's Best Dice Games; *Gil Jacobs.* Hundreds of dice games that reinforce a variety of mathematical skills.

Anno's Counting House; *Mitsumasa Anno.* Deals with numbers, addition, subtraction, sets and game theory.

Cat's Cradle; Owls, Eyes: A Book of String Games; *Camilla Gryski.* A collection of 40 string games is an introduction to math.

WRITING SPARKS

- Make a list of things that come in sets. Start with luggage and dishes and go from there. Choose a set to illustrate and display on a bulletin board **GET SET WITH SETS.**

- Write simple word problems using the list of sets. "You are going on a trip and need three suitcases. You have one. How many will you need to borrow?"

MORE TO EXPLORE

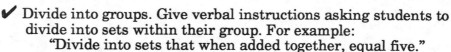
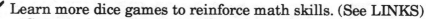

✔ Divide into groups. Give verbal instructions asking students to divide into sets within their group. For example:
  "Divide into sets that when added together, equal five."
  " Divide into sets of girls and boys."

✔ Learn more dice games to reinforce math skills. (See LINKS)
- Start with five dice. See which player can roll five of a kind on the fewest number of throws. Choose a number to be the one you are trying to roll. Then start counting rolls and times you see that number appear on the dice.
- Each player gets five rolls of the dice. The object is to score either the most or least points. Younger players may use a calculator. All players should have paper and pencil ready.
- Play this game with three dice. The object of the game is to be the first player to roll numbers totaling 10 or more. Score a point for each successful toss of the dice.

Color, cut and laminate for kit cover.
See preparation instructions, page 5.

Reproduce Page for Use in Student Kit

Rope a Problem

-- Cut and tape student directions inside kit. --

DIRECTIONS

1. You will need some scratch paper and a pencil to play this dice game.

2. Use the rope to make two circles next to each other.

3. Roll the dice near the yarn circles. Some will land inside the circles, some won't. Add the sets of dice in each circle. Then add the total of each circle together.

4. Pick up the dice and roll again.

5. Play with a partner to see who can find the answer the fastest.

Inventory Checklist

☐ 6 dice

☐ 2 pieces of yarn

• Count all the dice and put them back in the bag.

Things to Think About

• Were you able to add the numbers in your head or did you need to use paper?

• What other games could you play with dice that would help you practice your math? Think of one and teach it to a friend.

• Could you add more dice and rope circles to make this game harder?

Stop It!

> *Sometimes a minute flies by, sometimes it crawls. How long does it really take? Students will find out.*

SKILLS

- understanding the concept of time
- making comparisons
- fractions

PREPARATION

Materials:
- stopwatch

Directions:
1. Assemble all materials. Prepare the kit container and cover according to directions on page 5.

Student Preparation:
- Before introducing this kit to the classroom collection, demonstrate how to use a stopwatch. Allow students a chance to start, stop and reset the stopwatch.
- You might want to train one child in the use of the stopwatch. He or she could be the "teacher" students seek out with questions.

LITERATURE LINKS

A Minute is a Minute; *Barbara J. Neasi.* A minute can seem long or short—depending on what you're waiting for.

A Handful of Time; *Kit Pearson.* A young girl finds an old watch and is in for a surprise when she winds it.

A Seed, A Flower, A Minute, An Hour; *Joan W. Blos.* Tells of the ways in which things change, according to nature.

WRITING SPARKS

✎ Here are two time-related story starters ...
   - The longest minute of my life ...
   - My favorite hour of the day ...
   - It takes longer than you think to ...

✎ Make a list of time phrases we use in everyday speech— "Just a minute", "Hold on a second", "I've waited forever", "Time stood still"— are these phrases accurate expressions?

MORE TO EXPLORE

✔ Have this "time" game ready for classroom play and to build vocabulary. You'll need two categories of words—time divisions such as 15 seconds, 1 minute, one-half minute— and action words such as hop, wave, crawl. Write them on individual stips of tagboard and store separately in bags. Have your stopwatch or a timer with a second hand ready. Students choose a card from each bag and perform the action for the designated amount of time.

✔ Make a chart showing the progression of time from smallest unit to largest. Begin with millisecond and continue through second, minute, hour, etc.

✔ Use beans to create a visual picture of time. Count out a bean for every second in a minute, hour etc. Count again for minutes in an hour or a day, and again for hours in a day.

Color, cut and laminate for kit cover.
See preparation instructions, page 5.

-------------------------------------- Cut and tape student directions inside kit. --------------------------------------

DIRECTIONS
You will need a partner for these stopwatch activities.

1. Be sure you know how to start and stop the stopwatch before using this kit.

2. Your partner names an amount of time—for example " 15 seconds", "one minute"— then says "GO" and starts the stopwatch.

3. When you think that amount of time has passed, say "STOP".

4. Your partner stops the watch and tells you how much time has passed. How close were you?

5. Try again with another amount time. After a few turns, change jobs.

Inventory Checklist

❏ stopwatch

Things to Think About

• Does a minute take longer to pass than you thought?

• How long does it take to snap your fingers? blink your eyes? clap your hands?

• Were you able to count the seconds to help you figure out how much time had passed?

It's About Time

A travel clock provides students with the opportunity to learn about and practice telling time.

SKILLS

- telling time
- understanding a clock
- direction
- small motor development

PREPARATION

Materials:
- wind-up travel clock (not battery operated)
- clock patterns (page 93)

Directions:
1. Assemble all materials. Prepare the kit container and cover according to directions on page 5.
2. Cut apart and laminate clock patterns.

LITERATURE LINKS

The Tomorrow Book; *Doris Schwerin.* Introduces the concept of time.

Around the clock with Harriet; *Betsy & Giulio Maestro.* An elephant goes through the day's activities to help tell time.

The Backwards Watch; *Eric Houghton.* With a watch wound in reverse, a child and her grandfather go back in time to discover how much they have in common.

WRITING SPARKS

🖊 My favorite time of day is …

🖊 Give each student a clock pattern with a different time on it. Ask them to write about what they are usually doing at that time.

🖊 Story title: **The day that time stood still**

🖊 Go forward or back in time and create a character or describe an event.

MORE TO EXPLORE

✔ With permission from parents, bring in a variety of commonly used watches and clocks from home. These may include wrist and pocket watches, clock radios, cuckoo clocks, alarm clocks. Compare sizes, shapes and alarm sounds. Discover how each operates. Are they wind-up, battery-operated, solar, electric?

✔ Compare a digital clock and a standard clock with hands. Discuss the advantages and disadvantages of each.

✔ What is the difference between **A.M.** and **P.M.?** Brainstorm a list of activities that take place during each of these time divisions. As an individual project, fold a piece of paper in half. Label one half **A.M.** and the other **P.M.** Draw or cut and paste magazine pictures relating to those times of day.

✔ Discuss clockwise and counterclockwise and how it relates to a clock. Play a circle game. Call out direction; children move.

Color, cut and laminate for kit cover.
See preparation instructions, page 5.

Reproduce Page for Use in Student Kit

It's About Time

-------- Cut and tape student directions inside kit. --------

DIRECTIONS
Here are three things to try with the clock—and a partner

1. Set the clock to match all the time cards. Can you read the time as you set the clock?
Can you make the hands move in a different direction around the clock?

2. Set the clock to midnight. Set the clock to noon.
Are they the same or different?

3. Ask a partner to set the clock. Read the time.
Were you right? Trade jobs.

4. Ask a partner to name a time.
Set the clock to match. Trade jobs.

Inventory Checklist

☐ clock   ☐ 12 clock patterns

• Count the clock patterns to be sure that all
12 are back in the kit.

Things to Think About

• What do the hands on the clock mean? How do
they compare in size? Which is the second,
hour, minute hand? Is there a special hand for
the alarm?

• Why would you want an alarm clock?

• How does being able to tell time help you each
day? When do you need to know the time?

₡oupon ₡alculations

Money-saving grocery coupons provide the motivation for a variety of math computation plus lessons in saving and spending.

SKILLS

- addition and multiplication
- reading and interpreting a bar graph
- categorizing   • place value
- decimal point   • monetary value

PREPARATION

Materials:
- approximately 50 manufacturers coupons of assorted grocery and household items
- pencil
- paper

Directions:
1. Assemble all materials. Prepare the kit container and cover according to directions on page 5.
2. Clip colorful coupons from newspaper inserts and magazines.

LITERATURE LINKS

The Money Book and Bank; *Elaine Wyatt & Stan Hinden.* Gives children hands-on experience with saving and spending.

Make Four Million Dollars by Next Thursday; *Stephen Manes.* A young, would-be millionaire follows some crazy instructions to get rich quick—with some hilarious results.

Chicken Bucks; *Susan Sharpe.* Two enterprising children face financial challenges.

WRITING SPARKS

✎ Design a money-saving coupon for the product of your choice. Follow the format of the coupons in the kit. Cut and paste actual product pictures to add color and detail.

✎ Write a shopping list for a visit to the grocery store. Include items from the categories created in the graph below.

MORE TO EXPLORE

✔ Examine Sunday newspaper inserts with the class before clipping coupons. What types of products are offered? Make a bar graph to show ratio of: dairy products, cereals, dog and cat food, frozen food, soap, canned food, paper items.

✔ Brainstorm ways to save money. Think of ways to earn money too! (See LINKS)

✔ Take a poll to see how many parents save and use coupons on a regular basis. Do any parents have a special fund where they set aside money saved with coupons? What is done with the money saved? Ask families to keep track of money saved and share results.

✔ Practice shopping with the coupons. Use play money to calculate expenses, amount paid and change given. Figure out how much money was saved.

Color, cut and laminate for kit cover.
See preparation instructions, page 5.

Reproduce Page for Use in Student Kit

-------- Cut and tape student directions inside kit. --------

DIRECTIONS

1. Using all the coupons in the kit, close your eyes and choose five (5). Open your eyes and use these 5 coupons to calculate the following:
- the total saved if you used these 5 coupons the next time you shopped
- the total saved if the store <u>doubled</u> <u>the</u> <u>value</u> of each of these 5 coupons.

2. Try it again! Set these 5 coupons aside and select 5 new ones. Do the same calculations. Which set of coupons gave you the best value?

3. Sort all the coupons into categories.
- amount saved
- type of item (canned goods, cereal, cleaning supplies)

Inventory Checklist

❑ coupons

❑ pencil

❑ paper

Things to Think About

- Why do manufacturers offer coupons on new products?

- Why do manufacturers offer coupons on items people will buy anyway?

- Why would you want to use these coupons when you are shopping?

Let's Dine Out

Whet your appetite and get some mathematical practice with money and decimal points, too.

SKILLS

- computational skills
- reading and computing decimals
- recognizing monetary symbols
- reading monetary symbols

PREPARATION

Materials:

- food pictures cut from magazines. Select food that would be found on a restaurant menu.
- index cards
- sales pad (from a stationery store)

Directions:

1. Assemble all materials. Prepare the kit and cover according to directions on page 5.
2. Glue food pictures to index cards. Laminate.
3. Create a menu. Fold construction paper in half. Include the food items shown in the pictures. List a price for each one. Laminate.

LITERATURE LINKS

The Invitation; *Nicola Smee.* Leo wins a night out for his whole family at the swankiest restaurant in town.

Eats; *Arnold Adoff.* A mouth-watering, humorous collection of poems about food.

What's on the Menu? *Steve Goldsteen.* Experience the decision-making process when dining out and ordering from a menu.

WRITING SPARKS

- Create an original menu for a restaurant you are opening. Set prices. Write descriptions. Glue pictures. List by category.
- Have you ever eaten a memorable meal in a favorite retaurant? Describe it.
- What would you do if you didn't have enough money to pay for what you ordered and ate?

MORE TO EXPLORE

✔ Examine menus from different restaurants. Compare prices. Which items are most expensive? Which offer the best value? Is it more economical to order meals or a la carte? Do prices vary from one restaurant to another?

✔ Set up a mini restaurant in the classroom. Many skills can be practiced. Students can order *(reading)*, take orders *(listening)*, total the bill *(computation)*, pay the bill *(understanding monetary value)* and give change *(subtraction, decimals)*.

Color, cut and laminate for kit cover.
See preparation instructions, page 5.

Reproduce Page for Use in Student Kit

-- Cut and tape student directions inside kit. --

DIRECTIONS
Are you hungry? Get ready to "dine out" with a partner!

1. One person is the customer; one is the food server.
The customer needs the menu.
The food server needs the sales pad and food pictures.

2. Look atthe menu and decide what to order. Give your order to the server.

3. The server writes the order on the pad then selects the pictures ordered and serves the
meal to the customer. While the customer is "eating", the server totals the bill.

4. Change jobs. The customer is now the server. You can trade jobs as many times as you
want; just don't order the same thing each time.

Inventory Checklist

❑ food pictures   ❑ sales pad

❑ menu

• Tell your teacher if there are only a couple
pages left in the pad.

Things to Think About

• What things do you have to think about in a
restaurant **before** you order a meal?

• Do you like to eat in restaurants? Why? Why not?

• Take some time to read menus carefully. What
kind of restaurant is your favorite?

Calculator Kit

Children can learn a great deal by experimenting with calculators. Doors will open to new and more difficult mathematical operations.

SKILLS

- number operations
- number recognition
- mathematical symbol recognition
- budgeting

PREPARATION

Materials:
- calculator
- several catalogs
- grocery store advertisements
- calculator tapes from market purchases

Directions:
1. Assemble all materials. Prepare the kit container and cover according to directions on page 5.

LITERATURE LINKS

Focus on Calculator Math; *Charles Lund, Margaret Smart.* Activity resource.

Math Fun with a Pocket Calculator. *Rose Wyler & Mary Elting.* Teasers, tricks and games.

The Catalog; *Jasper Tomkins.* Three playful mountains receive a mail-order catalog and wind up buying more than they can handle.

The Way Things Work; *David Macaulay.* Pages 330-337 deal specifically with calculators.

WRITING SPARKS

- Pretend you are a famous scientist. What fantastic project are you working on that involves the use of a calculator?
- Write advanced number sentences ... with the help of a calculator.
- Make up word problems that can be solved with the use of a calculator.

MORE TO EXPLORE

- ✔ Encourage students to go grocery shopping with their parents one day and take along a calculator. Compute the cost of groceries as you shop. Practice multiplication by weighing fruits and vegetables and computing the cost. Determine the amount saved by using coupons.

- ✔ Calculators are needed for many jobs today. Interview parents to find out how they use calculators in their work. Make a list of the variety of uses. Discuss the benefits of using a calculator.

- ✔ Bring in a variety of calculators to share and examine. Compare the keys. Discuss the different operations on each. Find out how they operate. Encourage children to obtain a simple calculator to keep on hand at home for more calculations or for some classroom games.

Color, cut and laminate for kit cover.
See preparation instructions, page 5.

Reproduce Page for Use in Student Kit

-------------------------------------- Cut and tape student directions inside kit. -------------------------------------

DIRECTIONS
**Practice using a calculator to find out the answers
to some very hard problems.**

1. Pretend that you are shopping. Look through the catalogs and order whatever you want. Keep track of what you spend.

2. Go grocery shopping. Make a list how much you spent. How much would you spend in 4 weeks? in a year (52 weeks)?

3. Start with a very large number. Keep subtracting numbers until you get as close to zero as you can.

4. Choose one of the cash register receipts to add up again. Was it correct? Figure out the sales tax you would have paid in your state or province.

Inventory Checklist

- [ ] calculator
- [ ] catalogs,
- [ ] register receipts
- [ ] advertisements

- Turn off the calculator before putting it back in the kit.

Things to Think About

- How did the calculator make it easier for you to find answers to math problems?

- How could you or your parents use a calculator to help out around the house?

- When would it be a good time to use the calculator paper to print what you are punching

Shadow Show

Your friendly shadow—plus a few helpers— will teach you some lessons in measurement and light.

SKILLS

- measurement
- size comparison
- observation
- understanding the concept of light / dark

PREPARATION

Materials:

- flashlight
- ruler, measuring tape
- plastic fork, pencil, paper cup, pencil, small scissors, drinking straw
- thin white paper

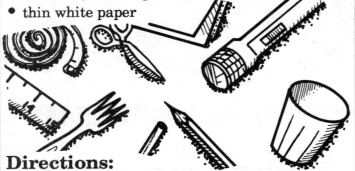

Directions:

1. Assemble all materials. Prepare the kit container and cover according to directions on page 5.

2. If the objects named above are not available, substitute and note the changes on the Inventory Checklist.

LITERATURE LINKS

Science Fun with a Flashlight; *Harriet Sherman.* Experimenting with light and shadow.

Shadow; *Blaise Cendrars.* Explores mysterious world of shadows. Caldecott medal winner.

The Biggest Shadow in the Zoo; *Parents Magazine Press.* Goober the elephant is upset when he thinks his shadow has drowned.

The Shadowmaker; *Ron Hansen;* A shadow maker tries to convince everyone that they need new shadows.

WRITING SPARKS

∅ One day my shadow came to life …

∅ Create silhouettes of student profiles. Write "profiles" —short, personal summaries— to accompany them.

∅ Describe what you like and dislike about daytime and nighttime. Research countries that have long days or nights.

MORE TO EXPLORE

✔ Draw animal shadows. Can classmates identify the animal?

✔ Head outside on a sunny day and work in pairs:
- Use chalk to trace your shadow. Measure. How do the shadows compare to actual height? Repeat at a different time of the day. Calculate the size differences.
- Use a piece of paper to cast a shadow over different objects. Measure the shadows. Compare.
- Play *Shadow Stompin'*. Try to step on each other's shadow.

✔ Make a shadow mural. Tack butcher paper to the wall. Set up a lamp. Hold objects up between the lamp and the wall. Trace the shadow on the butcher paper. Shadows can overlap. Paint.

✔ Observe the difference in vision capabilities in a well-lit versus a shaded or dark room. Measure how far you are able to see objects in each situation.

Color, cut and laminate for kit cover.
See preparation instructions, page 5.

Reproduce Page for Use in Student Kit

-------------------------------------- Cut and tape student directions inside kit. --------------------------------------

DIRECTIONS
You will need a partner to help you with these shadow activities.

1. Set a piece of white paper on the table in front of you. Hold a pencil in one hand and an object from the kit in the other hand.

2. Have your partner shine the flashlight over the object until it casts a shadow on the paper. Move the flashlight. Does the shadow change?

3. Use the pencil to trace the object's shadow. Measure the shadow and write its length next to it. Repeat this with all the objects in the kit.

4. Compare the measurements. Which object casts the longest shadow? the shortest? widest? Try the experiment again with the flashlight at a different distance from the object. Did the measurements change?

Inventory Checklist

- ☐ flashlight
- ☐ plastic fork
- ☐ paper cup
- ☐ drinking straw
- ☐ measuring tool
- ☐ pencil
- ☐ scissors

- Turn off the flashlight. If the light is dim, it may need new batteries.
- Add paper if needed.

Things to Think About

- Does moving the object closer to the flashlight make the shadow lighter or darker? Why?

- Can you see detail of the object in its shadow? Open and close scissors. Does the shadow move?

- Will an object cast a shadow if it is **behind** the flashlight? Try it to find out.

Balancing Act

Use a balancing scale to understand the concepts of measuring, estimating and comparing weight.

SKILLS

- comparing
- using measurement tools
- estimating
- problem solving

PREPARATION

Materials:
- balancing scale
- poker chips
- objects for weighing—suggestions are:
  - cup
  - detergent scoop
  - eraser
  - paper weight
  - candle
  - jar lid
  - shell/rock
  - toothbrush
  - sponge
  - salt or pepper shaker

Directions:
1. Assemble all materials. Prepare the kit container and cover according to directions on page 5.
2. Store the poker chips in a ziptop bag.
3. List the number of objects in the kit on the Inventory Checklist.

LITERATURE LINKS

The Balancing Girl; *Bernice Rabe.* A young girl confined to a wheelchair has a special skill for balancing. She uses her talent to benefit her whole school in an imaginative way.

Heavy Is a Hippopotamus; *Miriam Schlein.* A concept book about weight.

Hoboken Chicken Emergency; *Manius D. Pinkwater.* A mad professor with a 266-pound chicken save the day.

WRITING SPARKS

✐ How would you weigh an elephant? Illustrate an imaginative solution to this heavy problem!

✐ Make a list of the fruits and vegetables you could put in a grocery bag to equal 20 pounds—or the metric equivalent.

✐ Would you rather weigh as much as an elephant or as little as a mouse? Why?

MORE TO EXPLORE

✔ Take a trip to the grocery store and use the produce scales to weigh fruits and vegetables.

✔ Solve some silly problems. What would you use to balance the scales for an elephant ... a mouse ... a feather... Come up with some imaginative numbers and solutions.

✔ Cooperatively, make a list of animals. Estimate the weight of each. Students choose one to research for its actual (or approximate) weight. Get back together to share findings and compare with your estimates. Calculate the differences.

✔ Go outside and divide into teams for a "balance relay". Walk with a book on the head. Next put a ruler or stick on two fingers. Finally, balance a ball on a book.

✔ Make a chart showing the standards used to measure weight.

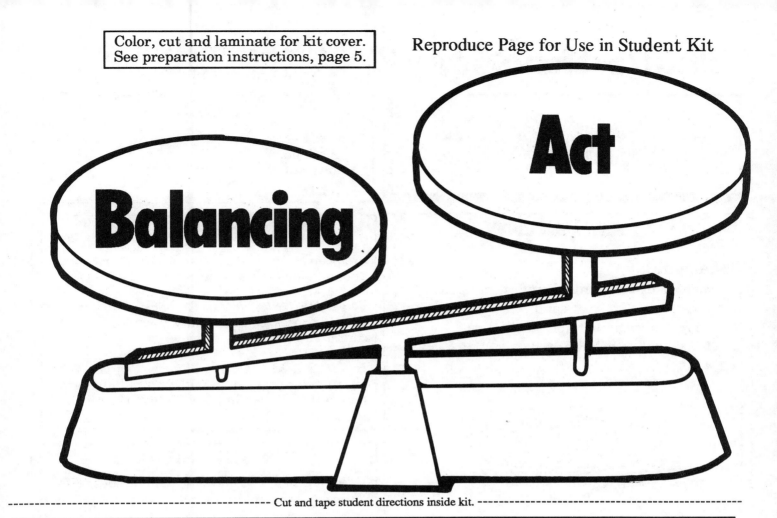

-- Cut and tape student directions inside kit. --

DIRECTIONS

Ask someone to show you how to use a balancing scale before you begin.

1. Take all the chips out of the bag.

2. Practice using the balancing scale.
   • Put three chips on one side. Put one chip on the other.
   • Do you see that the scale is tipped down lower on the side
      with the three chips?
   • Add two more chips to the other side. Do you see that the scales are now even?

3. Estimate how many chips you think it will take to balance each object in the kit. Test your estimates. Put each item on the scale and balance it with chips. Count the number of chips it took to balance the scale.

Inventory Checklist

☐ _____ objects for measurement

☐ poker chips

• Put all the poker chips back in ziptop bag.
• Count to be sure you have returned the correct number of objects to the kit.

Things to Think About

• Which object needed the **most** poker chips to balance the scale? Which needed the **least**?

• Were there any objects that weighed about the same? Which objects balanced?

• How could you use a balancing scale to measure pizza ingredients?

What's the Scoop?

It may not be ice cream but you can still enjoy scoops of another nature!

SKILLS

- making comparisons
- small motor
- understanding volume

PREPARATION

Materials:

- measuring scoop from laundry detergent
- cornmeal
- sand
- flour
- 3 large storage containers, with lids.
- 1 large tub to hold water
- 4 different sized tubs from margarine or other dairy products.

Directions:

1. Assemble all materials. Prepare the kit container and cover according to directions on page 5.
2. Clean out all tubs. Store and label the dry ingredients in three of them.

LITERATURE LINKS

Seashore Surprises; *Rose Wyler.* Discoveries abound along the seashore.

The Milk Makers; *Gail Gibbons.* Find out how milk is processed and finally measured into its containers of various sizes.

In The Night Kitchen; *Maurice Sendak.* Wild mixtures are measured and conjured up during a trip to the kitchen in the middle of the night.

WRITING SPARKS

✐ What other uses do we have for scoops? HINT: ice cream, building sand castles, bulldozers.

✐ Write **WHAT'S THE SCOOP?** stories. Here are two possibilities ... (See LINKS)
  - I was digging at the beach when I was amazed to see that I had scooped up ...
  - I was driving a bulldozer one day when I was surprised to scoop up ...

MORE TO EXPLORE

✔ Read recipe books. List the units of measurement used. Practice measuring tablespoons, teaspoons, cups. Convert the measurements to metric units.

✔ Choose a recipe to make. Follow the directions correctly. Then make the same recipe but do not measure the dry or liquid ingredients accurately. What differences were there in the results?

✔ Bring empty juice and milk containers from home. Read the cartons to find out the volume of liquid in each. Fill one of the containers with water. Empty it into another to compare amounts that each will hold.

✔ Compare the **weight** of a container filled with a liquid then a dry ingredient.

✔ Just for fun, use scoops, sand and water to construct a sand castle.

Color, cut and laminate for kit cover.
See preparation instructions, page 5.

----------------------------------- Cut and tape student directions inside kit. -----------------------------------

DIRECTIONS

1. Fill the empty container half way with water.

2. Have some towels ready to help with cleanup.

3. Use the different scoops and spoons to measure the flour, sand and cornmeal into each of the containers. Count the number of scoops or spoonfuls it took to fill each. Compare the results. Did it take more scoops to fill a container with flour than with sand?

4. Now use scoops and spoons to fill each container with water. Count each scoop. Did it take more or less or the same as the dry ingredients?

Inventory Checklist

❑ 3 containers filled with
  • flour • cornmeal • sand
❑ 1 empty container
❑ 1 scoop   ❑ 2 spoons

• Put the dry ingredients back in the right container and put the lid on tightly.
• Dry the container that had water in it.

Things to Think About

• How do we use scoops and measuring tools in our everyday life? Do you use scoops as toys or to dig? Do your parents use them to measure laundry soap or recipe ingredients? How do people use scoops in their jobs?

• Do you think a container can hold more water than flour? Why? Why not? What did you discover?

The BIG Cover-up

*Learn more about the size of things —
Introduce the idea of <u>covering</u> to teach
students the concept of **area**.*

SKILLS
- measurement
- size relationships
- concept of area
- predicting
- multiplication

PREPARATION

Materials:
- construction paper
- square potholder
- paperback book
- washcloth
- playing card
- paper towel
- large index card

Directions:
1. Assemble all materials. Prepare the kit container and cover according to directions on page 5.
2. Cut and laminate approximately 50 one-inch (2.54 centimeter) paper squares and 30- tree-inch (7.62 centimeter) paper squares. Store in separate bags.

LITERATURE LINKS

Area; *Shelley Freshman.* Young Math Series explores the concept of area.

Big Is So Big; *Bertha S. Dodge.* Explores different kinds of measurement.

Farmer Mack Measures His Pig; *Tony Johnston.* Two farmers are sure each one's pig is the biggest … and they're going to prove it!

WRITING SPARKS

▱ How would you measure the area covered by an elephant? Show your solution to this problem in a picture.

▱ Make a chart of 10 different items showing the area each covers from *least to most*. For example:
1. stick of gum
2. playing card
3. napkin
4. checker board
5. towel
6. throw rug

MORE TO EXPLORE

✔ Introduce students to TANGRAMS. Start a Tangram Library with each student contributing a puzzle of their own design.

✔ Work in pairs outdoors and use yarn to mark off an area on the playground. Record and count all items such as pebbles, insects, plants, found in the area. Try to predict how many of each item would be found in an area twice as large, 10 times as large, etc.

✔ Use graph paper for these activities:
  • Make designs or pictures that cover a certain amount of area.
  • Outline objects on the paper and compare the area each covers.

✔ Form a human perimeter. Walk-off the area from side to side. Change the size of the permieter and walk-off this new area.

✔ Consider the area of different things when answering questions such as "Which is larger, a baseball diamond or football field?"

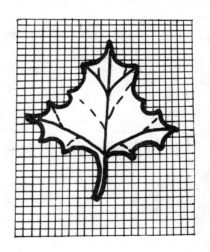

Color, cut and laminate for kit cover.
See preparation instructions, page 5.

Reproduce Page for Use in Student Kit

The BIG Cover -up

-------------------- Cut and tape student directions inside kit. --------------------

DIRECTIONS

1. There are two sizes of paper squares. Take them out of the bags but keep them in two piles!

2. Choose one of the items in the kit … the potholder, for example. Use the smaller squares to cover it completely. There shouldn't be any space between the squares. (Look at the picture for help.)

3. Count the number of squares it took to cover the **area** of the potholder. Write down the number. Now cover the potholder with the bigger squares. Count the squares and write the number.

4. Repeat this with all the things in the kit. Try to guess (predict) the number of squares —small and large—it will take to cover the area of each thing.

Inventory Checklist

- ❏ potholder
- ❏ paperback book
- ❏ index card
- ❏ two sizes paper squares
- ❏ playing card
- ❏ paper towel
- ❏ washcloth

- Be sure you put back 6 items.
- Separate the squares by size and put them back in the bags.

Things to Think About

- Which item used the most squares to cover it? Which used the least squares?

- Were your predictions close? Which number was easier to predict, the small or large squares?

- How many squares would it take to cover your desk? the classroom? a football field? What could you use to measure them

Tangle With an Angle

> *Angles are important not only in math but also in science, craft and design. Even the youngest students can learn to recognize and draw angles.*

SKILLS

- eye-hand coordination
- visual accuracy
- size comparisons
- developing a mathematical vocabulary

PREPARATION

Materials:

- straight edge
- pencil
- 4" diameter (10 cm) circle pattern
- crayons
- paper

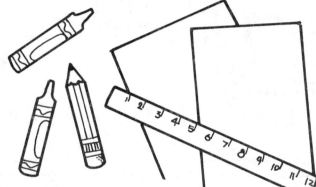

Directions:

1. Assemble all materials. Prepare the kit container and cover according to directions on page 5.
2. Cut the circle pattern from cardboard.

LITERATURE LINKS

Paper John; *David Small.* A mysterious fellow folds paper at different angles with some unusual and interesting results.

City: A Story of Roman Planning and Construction; *David Macaulay.* What roles do angles play in the planning of an imaginary Roman City. Clear pen-and-ink drawings provide some answers. Also by the author— ***Cathedral, Castle, Pyramid.***

WRITING SPARKS

- Make a BIG BOOK that illustrates, what you observed on your "angle expedition" (SEE MORE TO EXPLORE).Write simple copy. Older children might want to arrange for cross-age reading time with a younger class.

- Draw a geometric shape connected with angles. Write a story inside. Start with the sentence, **"Here's a new angle..."**

MORE TO EXPLORE

✔ Draw a variety of angles on the chalkboard. Ask students to recreate the angles on paper, from smallest to largest.

✔ Work together to make a large group mural consisting of colorful angles of various sizes.

✔ Go on an **ANGLE EXPEDITION.** Take a walk around school looking for angles. *Hints:* street intersections, building corners, lines in the sidewalk, tree branches.

✔ Build your angle vocabulary by writing these words on a large sheet of butcher paper tacked to the wall: *perpendicular, right, obtuse, intersect, acute, protractor.*

✔ Show interested students how to measure and draw angles using a protractor.

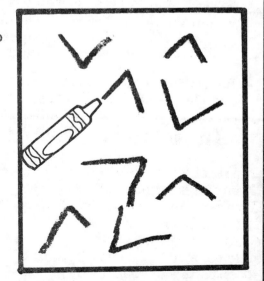

------ Cut and tape student directions inside kit. ------

DIRECTIONS
Here are two different activities to do to learn about angles.

Draw What You See
- Use a straight edge ruler and pencil and try to draw these angles on paper.
- Draw one more of each angle. Outline them with crayon to make a colorful picture.

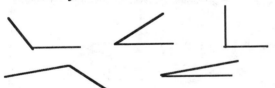

Make Some Paper Angles
- Trace two paper circles and cut them out. Make one cut from the outside to the center.
- Put the circles together as shown in the picture.

- Now turn them to make different sized angles.

Inventory Checklist

☐ straight edge ruler
☐ cardboard circle pattern
☐ paper   ☐ pencil   ☐ crayons

- Add more paper to the kit if you used the last piece.

Things to Think About

- Look around the room. Do you see any angles? What about where the walls meet the floor? Try to find others.

- Does a straight line all by itself form an angle?

- How could we put angles together to make a shape? Think of a triangle, a square or even a lot of pieces of apple pie!

43

Tasty Fractions

Here's a mouthwatering way for students to gain an understanding of fractions.

SKILLS

- understanding fractions
- problem solving
- identifying parts of a whole
- vocabulary development

PREPARATION

Materials:

- Tasty Fraction patterns & problem cards, pages 90-91.
- 4 small pie tins
- cardboard box
- construction paper—red, purple, blue, hot pink, orange, yellow

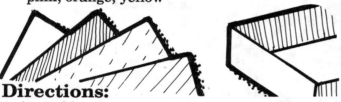

Directions:

1. Assemble all materials. Prepare kit container and cover according to directions on page 5.
2. Use the Tasty Fraction patterns to cut:
   - 8 cardboard pie wedges
   - 16 each—red strawberries, pink cherries, purple boysenberries, orange peach slices, blue blueberries, yellow lemon wheels
3. Laminate all fruit pieces and store separately in labeled, ziptop bags.
4. Cut apart and laminate problem cards.

LITERATURE LINKS

The Big Hungry Bear; *Don and Audrey Wood.* A lesson on sharing equally. A mouse shares a strawberry to keep it from the big hungry bear.

Eating Fractions; *Bruce McMillan.* Photographs of children eating parts of a whole (pizza, banana, etc.) introduces the concept of fractions.

Two Greedy Bears; *Jose Aruego.* Two bear cubs insis on sharing everything ... a folktale.

WRITING SPARKS

✐ Half the mice were happy, half the mice were sad. Why?

✐ Write about a time when sharing something equally was difficult for you to do.

✐ You've probably heard the questions "Is the glass half empty or half full?" Ask students to share their response. Read answers aloud and discuss.

MORE TO EXPLORE

✔ Make a wall chart of fraction terms. Include: bar, convert, denominator, numerator, improper, equal fractions, reduce, value. Use as a basis for a quick game of fraction trivia .

✔ Encourage kids to do some moon watching. Observe the shape of the moon—quarter, half, full. Track how long the changes take before the fractional cycle starts all over again.

✔ Play some "human fractions" games. Divide into teams. Call commands— "Divide into quarters." "Divide in half."

✔ Brainstorm a list of other ways we use fractions—referring to time, liquid and dry measurement. Practice:
- identifying parts of an hour
- pouring half a glass of water
- measuring half a cup of flour

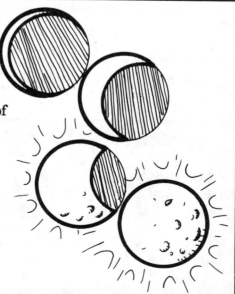

Color, cut and laminate for kit cover.
See preparation instructions, page 5.

Reproduce Page for Use in Student Kit

Tasty Fractions

-- Cut and tape student directions inside kit. --

DIRECTIONS
Serve some tasty pie and learn about fractions.

1. Pretend you are a waiter or waitress in a pie restaurant. Your customers' orders are on the cards.

Party of 4.

1/2 want lemon

1/4 want peach

1/4 want blueberry

The order tells how many people are at the table and what kind of pie, in fractions, they ordered.

2. Choose an order; then prepare the pie to take to the table. Fill the order and then prepare another.
- Choose the correct number of pie wedges.
- Put fruit on each wedge to equal the fraction ordered.

Inventory Checklist

☐ 8 cardboard pie wedges
☐ 6 bags of fruit—
   blueberries, strawberries, peaches, lemons, boysenberries, cherries
☐ 12 order cards

•Separate fruit and put back in their correct bag. Count order cards.

Things to Think About

- The word "fraction" means a part of something. If you eat part of a cookie, you ate a fraction of it. If you spent part of an hour playing, you played for a fraction of an hour. Can you think of other ways we use fractions to talk about what we do?

- Next time you dine out with your family, listen to what everyone orders. Then decide if the order could have been given in fractions.

Water Wowzers!

The shape of a drop of water creates a lens that magnifies what is underneath. Make water lens to explore this interesting concept.

SKILLS

- size comparison
- observation
- evaluation
- understanding magnification

PREPARATION

Materials:
For the water lens
- margarine tub
- rubber band
- clear plastic wrap
- scissors

For the kit
(7 small objects to examine)
- button
- small square of newspaper
- stone/pebble
- paper clip
- orange or lemon peel
- seed (any kind)
- cup hook
- eyedropper
- small cup

Directions:
1. Assemble all materials. Prepare the kit container and cover according to directions on page 5.
2. Make the water lens. See box above, right.

WATER LENS DIRECTIONS

- Cut an opening in the side of the margarine tub large enough for the thumb and index finger to fit and reach through.

- Stretch plastic wrap over the top of the tub.

- Hold in place with a rubber band.

LITERATURE LINKS

Something BIG Has Been Here; *Jack Prelutsky.* Huge animal tracks appear on the ground. Are they magnified or is an animal really that big?

Microscopes and Telescopes; New True Books; Childrens Press. Introduces the magnification cabilities of microscopes and telescopes. A challenge for older students.

MORE TO EXPLORE

✔ Take a walk armed with magnifying glasses. Start inside then head outside. Talk about your discoveries.

✔ Examine different parts of your body—your skin, fingernails, knuckles, knees—under a magnifying glass. What do you see?

✔ Find photograph books to share that show pictures of things magnified. Try to guess what the object in the picture is before revealing its identity.

✔ Set up a magnification center. Include magnifying glasses and microscopes. Encourage students to bring in objects to examine.

✔ Experiment with other clear liquids—soda water, vegetable oil, corn syrup— to compare their magnifying capabilities.

Color, cut and laminate for kit cover.
See preparation instructions, page 5.

Reproduce Page for Use in Student Kit

-- Cut and tape student directions inside kit. --

DIRECTIONS
Use a water lens to find out something interesting about a drop of water!

1. Put some water in the small cup.

2. Use the eyedropper to get some water from the cup. Put a few drops of water on the plastic wrap.

3. Carefully pick up one of the objects; the button for example. Look at it closely.
Gently reach through the hole in the tub and set the button inside the lens.

4. Look through the water drops on the plastic wrap and study the button again.
Does it look bigger? Take the button out and repeat the steps with all the other objects.

Inventory Checklist

☐ eyedropper ☐ small cup

☐ 7 objects

• Count the objects and to be sure all seven (7) are returned to the kit.
• Wipe the water off the plastic wrap.
• Dry out the small cup.

Things to Think About

• Did the holes in the button look larger? Did the print on the newspaper seem bigger?

• Could you see any details with the object in the lens that you couldn't see just looking at it?

• Why do you think that looking through water changes the size of something?

All Mixed Up

Mix and stir—Stir and mix. Sink, float or dissolve? Experiment with a variety of substances and observe how they interact with water.

SKILLS

- observation
- drawing conclusions
- compiling and recording data

PREPARATION

Materials:

- 6 plastic spoons
- 6 clear plastic cups
- 6 substances:
  - sand
  - sawdust
  - salt
  - sugar
  - flour
  - colored pencils
  - food coloring
- All Mixed Up data, page 89.

Directions:

1. Assemble all materials. Prepare the kit container and cover according to directions on page 5.
2. Store each substance in a labeled container. These will be consumed at the rate of one spoonful each per kit user.
3. Reproduce data log, page 89—One per kit user.

LITERATURE LINKS

Mouse Paint; *Ellen Stoll Walsh.* Three white mice do their share of mixing three pots of paint—red, yellow and blue.

Experiments with Water; New True Book Series; *Childrens Press.* Learn more about the properties of water.

Kitchen Chemistry; *Robert Gardner.* Challenge older students to learn more about the properties of liquids.

WRITING SPARKS

- **The Day I Dissolved**—Use this as a title to spark creative writing.

- How does the expression "water and oil don't mix" apply to people and friendships? Write a short paragraph interpreting this phrase. Read paragraphs aloud to spark discussion..

- Practice writing sentences that draw conclusions to scientific data.

MORE TO EXPLORE

✔ Use this simple experiment to practice recording data from an experiment and then translate the data into a graph or chart: Time how long it takes an ice cube to melt in three water temperatures—boiling, room temperature, iced.

✔ Here are some dissolving experiments that produce a tasty snack for all enjoy while you are discussing your observations.
- Make some gelatin salad. Experiment two ways—one with gelatin in boiling water and one in cold water.
- Dissolve cocoa in hot and cold milk. Conduct a taste test comparing the two procedures.
- Make some instant pudding. Record the changes as the powder interacts with the milk.

✔ And still one more experiment ... Dissolve other liquids in water. Try salad oil, corn syrup, coffee, tea, juice etc. Make a group chart that **illustrates** the results.

All Mixed Up

------- Cut and tape student directions inside kit. -------

DIRECTIONS
**What happens when a substance gets mixed with water?
Try it and find out.**

1. Fill each cup a little more than half way with water.

2. Put a spoonful of each substance and one drop of food coloring in different cups.

3. Just sit and watch for a minute. What do you see happening? Draw a picture of what you see in each cup on the top row of cups on the data page.

4. Now stir each mixture. Use a different spoon for each. Sit and watch for a moment. Draw a picture of what you see in each cup on the bottom row on the data page.

Inventory Checklist

☐ 6 containers of different substances including food coloring
☐ 6 plastic spoons   ☐ 6 plastic cups
• Dry each cup and spoon with a towel.
• Make sure the lids are on tight.
• Tell your teacher if you used the last of anything.

Things to Think About

• Do any of the things you mixed in the water seem to disappear?

• Which sink to the bottom? Which float to the top? Why do you think that happens?

• Do any seem to mix in but not disappear?

• What difference does stirring make, if any?

49

Air Dare

Air is all around us. Do you dare to learn more? This kit challenges children to do just that.

SKILLS

- observation
- problem solving
- application
- drawing conclusions

PREPARATION

Materials:

- large ziptop bag
- plastic cup
- straw
- hand-held paper fan
- cotton ball
- balloons

Directions:

1. Assemble all materials. Prepare the kit container and cover according to directions on page 5.
2. Make an accordion-folded paper fan if you prefer not to purchase one. Party shops usually carry inexpensive decorative fans.

LITERATURE LINKS

Air Is All Around You; Franklyn M. Branley.
Air, Air, Air; Lawrence Jeffries.
Both books provide questions, answers and simple experiments dealing with air.

The Red Balloon; Albert Lamorisse. A boy has a balloon best friend that follows him everywhere.

Busy O'Brien and the Great Bubblegum Blowout; Michelle Poploff. Boy has an inventive plan to raise money—a bubblegum blowout.

WRITING SPARKS

- One day I looked up and saw the most amazing thing floating through the air ...
- Brainstorm a list of ways we use air.
- Conduct an air experiment together. (See LINKS) Write a scientific report.
- Tell about the time you were carried through the air in a bubble to a surprise destination.

MORE TO EXPLORE

✔ Explore the ways air is felt. Stand in the wind, set up an electric fan, walk, run. Brainstorm other ways. Compare the effects.

✔ Look in a ray of sunlight to oserve the dust and other particles air carries. Discuss what can be carried through the air. Consider sound, seeds, pleasant or awful smells, smog, dust and gases.

✔ Conduct a problem-solving competition using air to move an object—a small plastic boat in a tub or water or a ping pong ball across the floor—from a starting point to a finish line. Students must devise a method. Award prizes (how about bags of air?) for the most inventive, fastest, most energy efficient.

✔ Does air have weight? Find out the answer together. Weigh a balloon. Blow it up and weigh it again. Conclusion?

✔ Fill up with air ... blow soap or bubblegum bubbles ... just for fun!

Color, cut and laminate for kit cover.
See preparation instructions, page 5.

Reproduce Page for Use in Student Kit

Air Dare

------------------------------- Cut and tape student directions inside kit. -------------------------------

DIRECTIONS
Here are four easy air experiments. Choose one or DARE to do them all!

BUBBLE TIME
Fill the cup half way with water. Use the straw to take a sip. As you suck, water will be pulled up. Why do you think this happens?

BIG BLOW UP
Toss the balloon in the air. What happens? Count how long it takes the balloon to land. Blow up the balloon. Ask someone to help you tie a knot. Toss the balloon in the air and count the landing time. Compare results.

IT'S INVISIBLE !
Hold the ziptop bag open and wave it through the air. Quickly seal it. What change do you see in the bag. How does it feel? Do you see anything inside?

FAN CLUB
Figure out a way to blow the cotton ball across the table top. You can blow on it or use the paper fan in the kit. Which way works the best? If you fan or blow harder is there a difference in how fast the cotton ball moves?

Inventory Checklist

- ☐ ziptop bag
- ☐ straw
- ☐ cotton ball
- ☐ plastic cup
- ☐ fan
- ☐ balloons

- Quietly let the air out of the balloon by poking a small hole. Throw it away.
- Wash and dry the cup and the straw.

Things to Think About

- What senses can you use to discover more about air? How do you feel it? Can you see it? Does it have a taste? Do you ever hear or smell it?

- If we had no air, how would we breathe? Would there be sound? How valuable is air to us?

- Air is *transparent*—it is clear. What else is transparent? Hint: plastic wrap, packing tape.

Noise Makers

This kit calls for what most kids like to do ...make noise!

SKILLS
- listening
- producing a variety of sounds
- sound comparisons
- learning the concept of vibration

PREPARATION

Materials:
- pencil, nail, chopsticks, toothpick
- jar lid, wooden block, plastic cup
- small plastic margarine tub

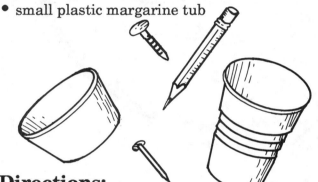

Directions:
1. Assemble all materials. Prepare the kit container and cover according to directions on page 5.

2. File the end of the nail so it is not sharp. Substitute a different metal object for younger kit users.

LITERATURE LINKS

Musical Max; *Robert Kraus.* A charming hippo can play any instrument ... and does ... much to the dismay of those around him.

Mr. Little's Noisy Car; A lift-the-flap book that explores the descriptive world of sound.

The Listening Walk; *Paul Shower.* A girl and her father go for a peaceful walk and discover the everyday sounds they've never listened to before.

WRITING SPARKS
- Compile a class list of words that describe sounds. Discuss the situations when you might hear that sound.
- Write a story that includes as many sounds as possible from the class list.
- Research and write about a musical instrument. Describe the sound it produces.

MORE TO EXPLORE

✔ Experiment with a variety of musical instruments. Compare the types of sounds you can create from each instrument. Try out drums, a triangle, xylophone and any others you might borrow from fellow musicians.

✔ Explore new sounds by tapping on various objects in the classroom, outside, and at home. Compare discoveries.

✔ Start a **CRAZY CLASS BAND.** Create sounds with everything from spoons to sandpaper. Plan a concert— for those brave enough to listen!

✔ Invent your own musical instruments from household items such as pot covers, rubber bands, coffee cans and bottles.

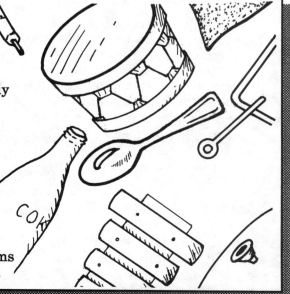

Noise Makers

-------------------------------- Cut and tape student directions inside kit. --------------------------------

DIRECTIONS
Discover the different sounds that objects make.

1. Tap the pencil on the jar lid. Listen to the sound. Now tap with the nail, then the chopstick and finally the toothpick. Do you hear any difference in the sound each makes?

2. Repeat the tapping of each object on the wooden block, the plastic cup and the margarine tub. Compare the differences you hear in the sounds.

3. Experiment with actions other than tapping. Hit the objects a little harder. Try scraping them. What changes, if any, do you hear?

4. Take a walk around the room and use the chopstick to tap on other objects. How many different sounds can you create?

Inventory Checklist

☐ pencil   ☐ nail   ☐ chopstick

☐ toothpick   ☐ lid   ☐ wooden block

☐ plastic cup   ☐ margarine tub

Things to Think About

• What words would you use to describe each sound?

• Which sounds were pleasant to listen to? Which were unpleasant? Why?

• What sounds can you hear at this moment?

• What is the difference between *noise* and *sound?*

Over the Rainbow

Rainbows are a fascinating sight to see. Create your own rainbow by converting white light to colored light.

SKILLS

- recording observations
- learning the order of colors in the spectrum
- graphing

PREPARATION

Materials:

- small glass prism*
- hand mirror*
- small pan or tub
- glass beads*

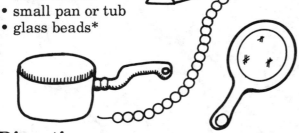

Directions:

1. Assemble all materials. Prepare the kit container and cover according to directions on page 5.
2. Prepare any glass samples so that there are no sharp edges. Wrap individual glass items in felt and in sealtop poly bags to prevent scratching and breakage.

* Discuss special handling for these delicate items.

LITERATURE LINKS

Sun and Light, *Neil Ardley.* Experiments with sun and light and easily available items show how the sun and light affect color.

Fun with Science—LIGHT, *Brenda Walpole.* Experiments, tricks, and things to make.

Skyfire; *Frank Asch.* When he sees a rainbow for the first time, Bear thinks that the sky is on fire and tries to put out the skyfire.

WRITING SPARKS

✎ Write acrostic poems about colors. Mount each on construction paper of the same color.

✎ What did you find at the end of the rainbow? Describe it.

✎ Write word lists—adjectives—that relate to the colors in a rainbow.

MORE TO EXPLORE

✔ What books can you find in the library that mention a rainbow? Set up a class display or read these books for story time.

✔ Plan a rainbow day and ask students to dress in their favorite colors. Can students form a rainbow of colors based on the order of colors in the spectrum?

✔ Do a class graph of favorite colors. What is the most popular color in the class? for girls? for boys?

✔ Paint rainbows showing the order of colors. (red, orange, yellow, green, blue, indigo, violet)

Color, cut and laminate for kit cover.
See preparation instructions, page 5.

Over the Rainbow

------------------------------- Cut and tape student directions inside kit. -------------------------------

DIRECTIONS

1. Try this experiment to make colored light (a rainbow) from white light. You will need to work on a sunny day near a window.

2. Fill the pan almost to the top with water. Set it on a table near the window. Prop up a mirror that is facing the window so that the sunlight hits the mirror and casts a rainbow on the ceiling.

3. Move closer to the window. Now move farther from the window. Do you see any changes?

4. Try this when the sun is high in the sky and try it again when it is low in the sky. What do you observe? Record your observations. Compare your findings with your classmates'.

Inventory Checklist

❑ glass prism ❑ small pan or tub

❑ hand mirror ❑ glass beads

• Empty the pan of water and dry the pan before replacing it in the kit.

• Wrap the glass prisms, beads and mirrors to prevent scratching or breaking.

Things to Think About

• What color do you see at the top of the rainbow? What is the order of colors from the top to the bottom?

• Is the order of colors always the same? Experiment with the glass or prisms and beads to find out.

• How else might you create a rainbow <u>outdoors</u> other than after a rain?

GET IT IN GEAR

Students become mini-machinists as they assemble a geartrain and observe the workings and movement of a gear.

SKILLS
- following directions
- observing
- drawing conclusions

PREPARATION
Materials:

- Three, 5" (12 cm) pieces of corrugated cardboard that is sandwiched between two smooth surfaces. Many cardboard cartons have this construction.
- Three brads or metal paper fasteners
- Empty thread spool or small wooden block
- Gear pattern (found on page 89)

This kit must be contained in a shoebox.

Directions

1. Assemble all materials. Prepare the kit container and cover according to directions on page 5.

2. Cut out the gear pattern on page 89. Trace and cut three gears from the cardboard. Punch a hole in the center of each gear.

3. Turn the shoebox upside down. Arrange the gears side by side so that the teeth interlock. (See diagram) Use a nail to punch a hole through the center of each gear **and** the box directly under it. Don't fasten the gears in place. The students will do that.

4. Glue an empty spool of thread or a wooden block anywhere on one of the gears to serve as a handle to help turn the gear.

MORE TO EXPLORE

✔ Observe how a handheld egg beater works. Note the horizontal and vertical gears. Use the beater to whip up some egg whites.

✔ Bring in simple items and toys from home that operate with the use of gears.

✔ Create a giant class geartrain using large and small gears. Color equal-sized gears the same color and make an eye-appealing bulletin board that really moves. Label it

"Gear up for Good Work"

✔ Explore the book *The Way Things Work,* written by David Macaulay. From levers to lasers, cars to computers, this book is a wonderful visual guide to the world of machines. Pages 40-51 deal specifically with gears.

Color, cut and laminate for kit cover.
See preparation instructions, page 5.

Reproduce Page for Use in Student Kit

-- Cut and tape student directions inside kit. --

DIRECTIONS

1. Put together a **geartrain.** Here's what to do. Take everything out of the shoebox and turn the box <u>upside down.</u>

2. Each circle with the **"teeth"** is a gear. Set the gears on the shoebox. Line up the hole in the center of each gear with a hole in the bottom of the shoebox.

3. When you have the holes lined up, put a metal fastener (called a "brad") through each gear and the hole under it. Reach under the box and spread open the "arms" of the brad. This should keep the gears from falling off the box.

4. Turn the handle on the gear. You may need to adjust the brads for the gears to move freely.

Inventory Checklist

☐ 3 gears
☐ 3 brads

• Take apart the geartrain .

•Tell your teacher if the brads need to be replaced or the knob has fallen off.

Things to Think About

• How does a gear affect the movement of a smaller gear next to it? Do the gears move at the same speed? Why are several called a **geartrain**?

• How would a broken "tooth " affect a geartrain?

• What do the terms **clockwise** and **counter clockwise** mean? Watch the movement of each gear when you change directions.

FUN with FRICTION

Discover how friction comes to the rescue in school, at home, on the playground...just about everywhere!

SKILLS

- to learn what causes friction
- drawing conclusions
- application

PREPARATION

Materials:

- 2 shingles
- 2 smooth, sanded pieces of wood
- cotton balls
- plastic gloves (to prevent splinters
- visit the local lumberyard and ask for leftover cuttings of lumber

Directions:

1. Assemble all materials. Prepare the kit container and cover according to directions on page 5.

LITERATURE LINKS

Making Things Move; Neil Ardley. Friction experiments and activities.

Friction All Around; Tillie Pine & Joseph Levine. Illustrates everyday objects and occurences causing friction.

Who Is The Beast?; Keith Baker. There's friction deep in the jungle! Can the animals solve their differences and become friends?

WRITING SPARKS

✎ Describe the imaginary town of "Slipperyville" where there is no friction. Collect all the stories and title the class collection **No-Friction Fiction.**

✎ Create a cartoon character "Friction Man" or "Friction Woman." Tell how he or she saves the day by using friction in an important and unusual way.

MORE TO EXPLORE

✔ Start a class list of Friction Findings, telling how friction helps us in school and at home. (For starters: a match can be lit, pencil writing can be erased, jars can be opened, etc.) Encourage student demonstrations of those that are safe.

✔ Discuss safety precautions to prevent slipping and skidding. What is the purpose of special athletic shoes? Why do cars use chains or snow tires in the snow?

✔ Go on a school or home hunt to look for smooth and rough surfaces. Which ones are smooth and easy to slide on? Which ones are rough and difficult to slide on?

✔ Conduct tests with fine-grained sandpaper. Test friction with a rough surface, sand, then test again. Discuss the differences.

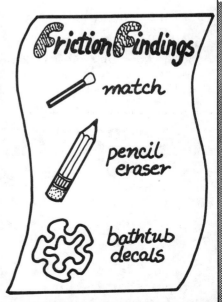

Color, cut and laminate for kit cover.
See preparation instructions, page 5.

Reproduce Page for Use in Student Kit

FUN with FRICTION

Cut and tape student directions inside kit.

DIRECTIONS

Try this activity to see how you can make things slide more easily. Use the plastic gloves to prevent getting splinters!

1. Select two pieces of rough wood and slide one piece over the other. Repeat the action with the smooth wood. What do you observe?

2. Pull a cotton ball across the rough wood. What happens? Now pull it across the smooth wood.

3. Attempt to slide both kinds of wood over a carpeted area. What happens?

4. Find other surfaces—cloth, upholstery, cement—on which to conduct friction tests.

Inventory Checklist

☐ cotton balls   ☐ rough wood pieces

☐ plastic gloves   ☐ smooth wood pieces

☐ soft cloth

Things to Think About

• What other ways can you make things slide or move more easily?

• What are some common "lubricants" that help to reduce friction?

• How does sand on a roadway help on a snowy day?

• Why are Rollerblades so easy to skate on? How does friction help you to stop?

59

Weather or Not!

Students try their hand at reporting the weather as they learn how to observe and measure temperature changes.

SKILLS

- observation
- reading a thermometer
- vocabulary development
- oral language

PREPARATION

Materials:

- copies of paper thermometer, see page 87
- one outdoor thermometer
- red marker or crayon
- wall map of U.S., Canada or your region (optional)

Directions:

1. Assemble all materials. Prepare the kit container and cover according to directions on page 5.
2. Mount the outdoor thermometer outside your classroom at a height that is convenient for students to read.
3. Reproduce thermometer—(page 87)—one page per student.

LITERATURE LINKS

Cloudy With a Chance of Meatballs; Judith Barrett. Read about the crazy changes in weather in the land of Chewandswallow.

Eyewitness Books: Weather; Brian Cosgrove. Find out the causes of weather changes and why weather forecasters are seldom 100% right.

It's Raining Cats and Dogs: All Kinds of Weather and Why We Have It; Franklin M. Branley. Strange happenings such as pink and green snowstorms are mixed in with scientific accounts of the weather.

WRITING SPARKS

✎ Make a list of weather-related words. Use them to describe the weather conditions each day.

✎ Use "weather words" to describe your personality.

✎ Let me tell you about the day it didn't rain water but rained...

MORE TO EXPLORE

✔ Watch weather reports on the major TV stations in your area. What elements of the weather are used in their reporting?

✔ Invite students to act as the day's weatherperson and report the weather. Use a wall map to report weather across the country.

✔ Make a bar graph that is filled in daily based on high temperatures for a given period: one week, two weeks, a month. What was the high temperature for the entire period?

✔ Compare the weather where you live to the rest of your state (province) or country. How does it change each season?

✔ Learn to convert Fahrenheit and Celcius temperature readings.

✔ Learn to look for and read weather reports in the newspaper.

Color, cut and laminate for kit cover.
See preparation instructions, page 5.

Reproduce Page for Use in Student Kit

Weather or Not!

------- Cut and tape student directions inside kit. -------

DIRECTIONS

1. Look at the thermometer outside your classroom. Use one copy of the paper thermometer to record your findings by making a red line on the paper.

2. Fill in the thermometer with a red crayon or marker to show the temperature.

3. Note other weather features of the day and check these.

4. Practice reading the thermometer and saying the temperature in degrees.

5. Repeat this two more days. When you have all three thermometers marked, figure out the difference in degrees from day to day.

6. If you wish, practice your weather report to recite to the class. You may use your notes!

Inventory Checklist

❏ copies of paper thermometer

❏ red marker or crayon

• Please be sure the cap is on the marker!

Things to Think About

• How do the following people use thermometers? cooks, doctors, butchers, bakers?

• What does the liquid in the thermometer do when the temperature goes up? when the temperature goes down?

• What words can you use to describe weather?

HOW DENSE!

Sink or Swim? Experiment with a variety of objects in a tub of water to observe their density.

SKILLS

- observation
- drawing conclusions
- hypothesizing
- visual perspective

PREPARATION

Materials:

- 12 different objects. These are suggested but any can be substituted.
  - marble • cork • sponge • wooden block
  - stone/pebble • plastic drinking straw
  - bolt • plastic spoon • rubber band
  - metal spoon • ping pong ball • eraser

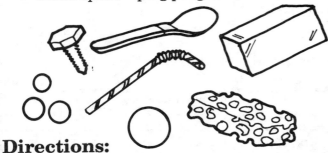

Directions:

1. Assemble all materials. Prepare the kit container and cover according to directions on page 5.

SPECIAL NOTE:
   Use a clear plastic shoebox or other see-through container for the kit.

LITERATURE LINKS

Scuffy the Tugboat; *Gertrude Crampton.* A small toy boat floats out to sea with many adventures along the way.

The Riddle of the Floating Island; *Paul Cox.* Trail of missing objects leads to a floating island.

Density is the mass—the amount of matter—of any substance. Density can be measured by floating an object in water. Its density is equal to the percentage that is submerged.

WRITING SPARKS

- Describe the adventures of a toy rubber tugboat that floats out to sea.

- Write descriptions from two different perspectives; pretend you are floating on the ocean. Then describe what you saw when you sank to the bottom.

MORE TO EXPLORE

✔ Compare the relationship of an object's weight to its ability to float. Draw conclusions about the relationship of weight to density.

✔ Compare how water level is affected by the density of an object. Pour water into a clear plastic cup. Measure the level. Drop in an object and measure the level again.

✔ Compare density by categories—metal, plastic, wood—Is any category denser on the whole than another?

✔ Conduct density races with a variety of liquids. Pour an equal amount of salad oil, water, soda, molasses, for example, into clear containers. Drop a marble into each and time the marble's trip to the bottom. Compare the results and draw conclusions. Write a scientific report together.

Color, cut and laminate for kit cover.
See preparation instructions, page 5.

Reproduce Page for Use in Student Kit

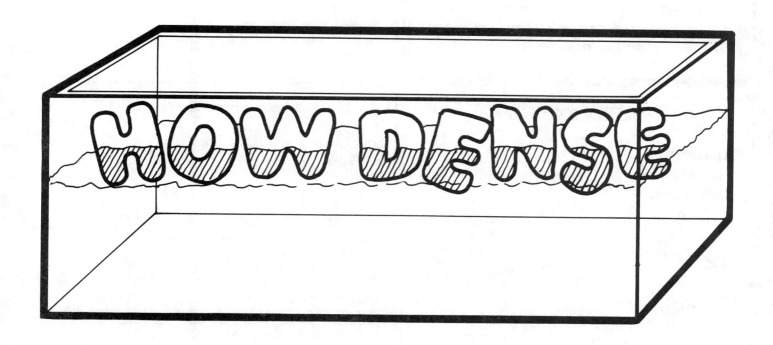

-- Cut and tape student directions inside kit. --

DIRECTIONS
Sink or float? Find out!

1. Take all the objects out of the kit. Fill the kit half way with water.

2. Pick up the objects one at a time. Feel the weight and shape. Which objects do you think will sink? Which do you think will float?

3. Set each object in the water. Start by putting them in one at a time. Look through the side of the kit. Observe how much of an object is below the water. Did it sink all the way to the bottom?

4. Set several objects in the water at the same time. Look through the side of the kit and compare the differences.

5. Line up all the objects in order from the ones that sank to the ones that floated.

Inventory Checklist

• Count the objects to be sure you return 12 to the kit.

• Dry the kit with a towel before you put the things back in it.

Things to Think About

• Do you think that the weight of an object has anything to do with it sinking or floating?

• Did the size of an object make a difference in its ability to float?

• Were the objects that you thought would float the ones that really did? How close were your guesses?

MOON JUMPING

The concept of gravity will be much easier to visualize after students practice "moon jumping"!

SKILLS

- measurement
- addition or multiplication
- concept of gravity

PREPARATION

Materials:
- piece of chalk
- tape measure
- multiplication chart**(optional)

Directions:
1. Assemble all materials. Prepare the kit container and cover according to directions on page 5.

LITERATURE LINKS

Weight and Weightlessness; *Graham Booth.* Clear text and appealing illustrations explain weightlessness.

The Magic School Bus: Lost in The Solar System; *Joanna Cole.* Students on the magic school bus get a close-up look at the moon ... and outer space.

First Travel Guide to the Moon: What to Pack, How to Go, What to See When you Get There; *Rhoda Blumberg.* Intro to the moon.

STUDENT PREPARATION

Define and discuss **gravity.** Gravity is the attraction of the earth's mass for objects near its surface. The greater the gravitational attraction, the less an object can jump.

WRITING SPARKS

✍ Imagine that you could jump as high as if you were on the moon. What advantages or disadvantages would you have?

✍ Describe how it would feel to walk on the moon without heavy equipment to hold you down.

✍ Make a list of the sports that would be affected if athletes could jump as if they were on the moon.

MORE TO EXPLORE

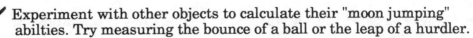

✔ Experiment with other objects to calculate their "moon jumping" abilties. Try measuring the bounce of a ball or the leap of a hurdler.

✔ A boy or girl who weighs 60 pounds on earth would weigh only 10 pounds on the moon. Calculate student weight if they were on the moon.

✔ Find out about how astronauts were able to walk on the moon. What affect did their heavy equipment have on their ability to move around?

✔ Find out why gravity is weaker on the moon. (It is because the moon's mass is 81 times smaller than the earth's mass.) Make a chart showing the gravity of other planets compared to the earth—and the moon.

Reproduce Page for Use in Student Kit

Color, cut and laminate for kit cover. See
preparation instructions, page 5.

-------------------------------------- Cut and tape student directions inside kit. --------------------------------------

DIRECTIONS

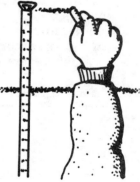

1. With chalk in your hand, stand with your side against a wall. Reach your hand as high as you can and make a small mark on the wall. (If you cannot make a mark on the wall, have a partner "mark" the spot for you.)

2. Standing in the same spot, jump up in the air and make another mark as high as you can.

3. Measure the distance between the lines. This is how high you jumped.

4. Multiply this distance by **six.** If you can't multiply, add the number six times.

THIS IS HOW HIGH YOU COULD JUMP IF YOU WERE ON THE MOON.
For example, if you jumped one foot (30 cm) you would be able to jump six feet (180 cm) on the moon!

Inventory Checklist

☐ piece of chalk

☐ tape measure

• Be sure you wipe the chalk mark off the wall where you jumped. Use a soft rag or paper towel.

Things to Think About

• Compare your jump with a classmate's. What were the differences between your first jumps and your "moon" jumps?

• Do you know why 6 is the magic number? It is because the moon's gravity is one-sixth as great as the earth's.

• Imagine jumpers like a kangaroo or grass-hopper. How high could they could jump on the moon?

HAVE A BALL

TEACHING GUIDE
Preparation Notes

The simple bounce of a ball may hold some surprises for young scientists.

SKILLS
- listening • observing • predicting
- drawing conclusions
- experimenting with gravity
- understanding size/weight relationships

PREPARATION

Materials:
- 5-7 balls of *different* sizes and weight. Some suggestions are: marble, golf, tennis, ping pong, nerf, and racquet balls. Check your local drug stores for party-favor balls, too.

Directions:
1. Assemble all materials. Prepare the kit container and cover according to directions on page 5.
2. Note the number of balls in the kit on the student inventory list.
3. Use a permanent marker to number each ball.

LITERATURE LINKS

Gravity Is a Mystery; Don Madden. Illustrates gravity's effect on life.

The Ball Bounced; Nancy Tafuri. A bouncing ball causes much excitement around the house.

The Mystery of the Magic Green Ball; Steven Kellogg. A frustrating search for a favorite green ball ends with a surprising turn of events.

Balls; Susan Morrison. History and description.

WRITING SPARKS

✐ Report on one of the experiments in the kit. Include: problem statement, materials used, observations, conclusions.

✐ Imagine that you bounced a ball and it never came down. Where did it go? What happened to it? Did it *ever* come down?

✐ Write a paragraph describing an experiment conducted by one of the scientists listed.

MORE TO EXPLORE

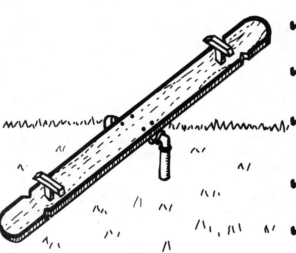

✔ Report on the gravity experiments conducted by Galileo, Newton and Einstein.

✔ Find out how earth and the other planets in the solar system are affected by *gravitational pull.*

✔ What will interfere with gravity? Conduct some tests. Heat the balls in water. Freeze them. Blow them with a fan while dropping them. Any changes?

✔ Make a line graph that shows the results of the height each ball bounced.

✔ Learn about the *center of gravity.* Take a trip to the playground teeter-totter, walk a "tightrope" stretched on the ground, experiment with a balancing scale.

Color, cut and laminate for kit cover.
See preparation instructions, page 5.

Reproduce Page for Use in Student Kit

HAVE A BALL

------ Cut and tape student directions inside kit. ------

DIRECTIONS
A ball bounces because of <u>GRAVITY</u>. Here are two experiments to try.

LOOK

1. Look at all the balls in the kit. Pick each one up. Which one do you think will <u>bounce</u> the highest? Write their numbers in that order.

2. Now bounce each ball. Don't use force. Hold them from the same spot in front of you before you drop them. You may work with a partner to help keep track of how high each ball bounces. Write their numbers in order. Compare it to your list.

3. Hold the balls at a different height and repeat the experiment. Were the results different?

LISTEN

1. Do you think the balls will fall to the ground at the same time? Find out.

2. Choose two (2) balls and hold them out in front of you, one in each hand Close your eyes and listen carefully while you drop the balls at the same time. Did you hear the balls hit the ground? Did the balls land at the same time?

3. Repeat the experiment with the balls at a different height. Now try it with two other balls.What do you hear each time?

Inventory Checklist

☐ ____ balls

• Count the balls to make sure you have the correct number before putting the kit away.

Things to Think About

• How close were your guesses in the **LOOK** experiment. Did the ball that bounced the highest surprise you? Did weight make a difference? Did size? If you aren't sure, hold each ball again and look at its place on the list.

• Did you think the balls would hit the ground at the same time ? They fell at the same speed because of **gravity.**Could you do anything to

STAR GAZERS

Become a star gazer! Students create a mini-planetarium that will enable them to view the shape of the constellations.

SKILLS

- visual memory
- small motor
- application
- fact finding

PREPARATION

Materials:

- half-sheets, black construction paper
- constellation pattern, page 88
- straight pins

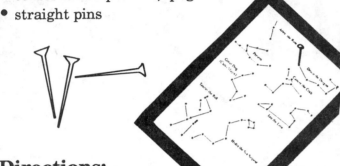

Directions:

1. Assemble all materials. Prepare the kit container and cover according to directions on page 5.
2. Reproduce constellation pattern, page 88— one per student using the kit.
3. Staple a pattern page at each corner to the black construction paper.
4. Store the pins in a closable case or ziptop bag.

LITERATURE LINKS

The Sky is Full of Stars; Felicia Bond. Learn about star colors and brightness and locating major constellations.

Look to the Night Sky; Seymour Simon. An introduction to star watching.

The Sun: Our Nearest Star; Don Madden. Simple discussion of the sun and its benefits.

Shooting Stars; Holly Keller. Explains these complex, luminous objects.

WRITING SPARKS

✐ Story title: **My Ride on a Shooting Star**

✐ If you could make a wish on a star, what would it be?

✐ Write ten facts about the sun, our nearest star, on index cards.
  - Use them in a game of trivia.
  - Link them together for an oral presentation.

MORE TO EXPLORE

✔ Make a classroom **planetarium.** Provide groups of students with dark blue or black butcher paper. Use glow-in-the-dark paint to recreate constellations. Hang the paper like a canopy from the ceiling. Push back the desks, lay on the floor, turn off the lights and do some star gazing.

✔ Heavily color yellow shooting stars. Paint a blue or black watercolor wash over the stars.

✔ Encourage students to spend part of an evening gazing at the stars. Determine which stars seem brighter. Try to locate constellations.

✔ Make a graph that shows the distance in light years to six or more stars.

Color, cut and laminate for kit cover.
See preparation instructions, page 5.

STAR GAZERS

-------------------------------- Cut and tape student directions inside kit. --------------------------------

DIRECTIONS
Make your own star gazer.

1. Carefully choose a straight pin and a constellation pattern to use.

2. Lay down on a carpeted area to do this project.
   Set the construction paper on the floor, pattern side up.

3. Poke a pin through each star, all the way through both papers.
   Read the names of the constellations (groups of stars) as you work.

4. When you have finished poking the pin through all the dots,
   turn your paper over and hold it up to a light or bright window.

Do you see the constellations?

Inventory Checklist

☐ pins
☐ constellation patterns

• Tell your teacher if the kit needs more constellation patterns.

• Put the pin back in its container.

Things to Think About

• Can you name the constellations? Turn your paper over if you can't remember.

• Why do you think the constellations were given their names?

• Are there nights when the stars seem brighter than other nights? Why? Are some stars brighter than others? Why?

Compass Capers

How would you find your way if you had no landmarks and no sun? Discover one of history's most helpful inventions.

SKILLS

- directionals
- fact integration
- histoical perspective
- analysis

PREPARATION

Materials:
- compass
- paper
- pencil

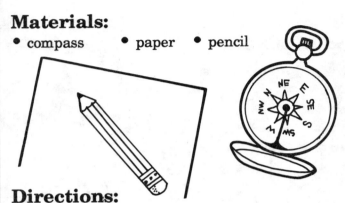

Directions:
1. Assemble all materials. Prepare the kit container and cover according to directions on page 5.

Background Information:
The essential part of a magnet compass is a strip of magnetized steel supported on a pivot so that the strip can swing freely. Under the influence of the earth's magnetic field, the needle of a compass comes to rest in a north-south position.

LITERATURE LINKS

The Compass; (Inventions That Changed Our Lives); Paula Hogan. Traces the history of the compass from its invention to modern day.

The Compass in Your Nose and Other Astonishing Facts About Humans; Marc McCutcheon. Interesting anatomical facts.

North, South, East and West. Robert Galster. Learn compass directions using your shadow.

South and North, East and West; Michael Rowen. Cultural stories from all over the world.

WRITING SPARKS

- Write a new ending to the standard fairy tale Hansel and Gretel using a compass instead of breadcrumbs.
- Look at a map of your country. Choose a state or province in the north, south, east or west to write about. Make a map that shows the boundaries in each direction..

MORE TO EXPLORE

✔ Plan a walking field trip to a community destination. Make a map—block by block from the school to the site—which shows the direction, north, south, east or west, to turn at each corner. Try to borrow enough compasses for small groups to share.

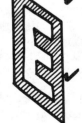

✔ Make directional signs to show N-S-E-W in the classroom. Answer questions and give instructions relating to these signs. "Put your stories in the baskets along the north wall."

✔ Compasses have been used throughout history by sailors, explorers, aviators, astronomers and now motorists. Divide into groups to write and present short historical skits choosing one of these groups.

✔ Go outside to determine direction using the sun. (It rises in the east and sets in the west.)

Color, cut and laminate for kit cover.
See preparation instructions, page 5.

Reproduce Page for Use in Student Kit

Compass Capers

-- Cut and tape student directions inside kit. --

DIRECTIONS

1. Set the compass on top of the paper so that the needle swings freely.

2. With a pencil, make lines on the paper as if you were making the needle longer at both ends. Look at the picture for help.
   Leave the compass in place and draw a circle around it.

3. Pick up the compass, turn it a little and put it back on the paper in the circle you just drew.
   What do you notice about the needle?
   Pick it up and move it again. Any changes?

4. Carry the compass and take a walk around the room .

Inventory Checklist

☐ compass
☐ paper   ☐ pencil

• Add more paper if you used the last piece.

Things to Think About

• Why doesn't the needle ever point in a different direction? (It always points to the north.)

• How do we use the letters on the compass to help us find our way?

• Have you ever been lost? Would a compass have helped you?

TELEPHONE TALK

TEACHING GUIDE
Preparation Notes

The "walkie-talkie" of yesterday may be old hat to adults but can be a fun new source of learning for students about how sound travels.

SKILLS
- listening
- concept of how sound travels
- cooperative learning
- vocabulary development

PREPARATION

Materials:
- 10 feet (3 meters) of string
- 2 sturdy paper or styrofoam cups

Directions:
1. Assemble all materials. Prepare the kit container and cover according to directions on page 5.

2. Make a small hole in the bottom of each cup. Insert each end of the string through a cup hole. Tie a large knot or tape the string securely so it will not loosen or pull through the hole when stretched taut.

LITERATURE LINKS
Sound; *Keith Brandt.* Easy explanations relating to human voices and what causes sound to be heard.

High Sounds, Low Sounds; *Crowell.* Describes the process by which vibrations become meaingful sounds. Simple experiments using household items show how sounds are produced and carried through the air.

WRITING SPARKS
- Write five silly or scary sentences to speak into the cup. The student listening writes down (or repeats) what was heard.
- Make up a class list of clever, catchy names for these string telephones. Vote for the class favorite.
- Write a scrpit for a telephone conversation. Ask classmates to roleplay the conversation.
- Research the invention of the telphone and its inventor, Alexander Graham Bell.

MORE TO EXPLORE

✔ Experiment with making string phones from other items such as cereal boxes, and milk cartons. Compare the results.

✔ Research the experiment conducted by French scientist Jean Baptiste Biot in which he used the water pipes of Paris at a time when all the water had been drained out of them.

✔ Make a megaphone by rolling construction paper into a wide cone with one opening small and the other wide. Demonstrate the effects of using a megaphone to concentrate the sound of a voice in one direction.

✔ Find out how a telegraph works. Learn about Morse Code. Send a telegram to the class.

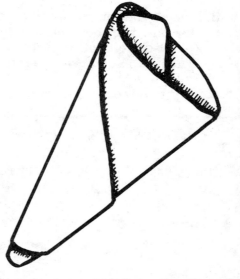

-------------------------------------- Cut and tape student directions inside kit. --------------------------------------

DIRECTIONS
Work with a partner and the string telephone to find out how sound travels.

1. Each person holds a cup. Moving slowly so as not to tangle the string, walk away from each other until the string is stretched straight between you.

2. One person holds the open end of a cup to his or her ear. The other person talks into the open part of the cup. Be sure the string is not touching anything while the phone is in use.

Inventory Checklist

☐ two cups connected by a string.

• Roll the string carefully around your fingers to keep it from getting tangled. before you put it back in the kit.

• Tell your teacher if the cups are getting bent and need to be replaced.

Things to Think About

• What happens when you speak with the string **pulled tight?** with the string **touching** something? with someone **pinching** the string?

• How does sound travel from one cup to the other? Look up <u>vibration</u> in the dictionary.

• How does the string phone compare to modern telephones? What causes interference on a telephone line?

REFLECTIONS

Students will enjoy colorful tricks as they discover how something they use daily—a mirror—works to produce images.

SKILLS

- to understand the concept of reflection
- to understand how a mirror works
- observation
- drawing conclusions

PREPARATION

Materials:

- 3 equal-sized hand mirrors
- tape   • button   • penny
- bits of brightly colored paper
- half sheet white drawing paper

Directions:

1. Assemble all materials. Prepare the kit container and cover according to directions on page 5.

2. Tape the three small mirrors as shown at right. Reflective side faces **inward.**

3. Store colored paper in a ziptop poly bag.

LITERATURE LINKS

My Mirror; *Kay Davies, Wendy Oldfield.* Uses simple activities with a mirror to introduce basic science concepts.

Talk About Reflections; *Angela Webb.* Discusses reflections. Includes photographs.

Bouncing and Bending Light; *Barbara Taylor.* Projects and experiments demonstrating the effects of mirrors and lenses on rays of light..

WRITING SPARKS

🖋 Write Kaleidoscope rhymes. Start with a color and use short phrases describing things that remind you of that color.

🖋 Describe a kaleidoscope.

🖋 Describe what would be seen in a mirror if it were reflecting your bedroom.

🖋 List the times that you use a mirror.

MORE TO EXPLORE

✔ Examine an old or inexpensive hand mirror that shows the silver peeling off the back. Or, scratch the silver off and show how light reflects when it hits a mirror.

✔ This activity illustrates *left-right reversal* in a mirror. Write the number 81 with a crayon on a piece of paper and hold it up to a large mirror. What number is seen in the mirror (18)? Copy this number and hold it up in the mirror. Presto! It's 81 again. Let children try with different numbers. What do they discover?

✔ Go on a **REFLECTION WALK.** Look for other objects in which children can see their reflection. Ask them to hunt at home and in the classroom, too. What conclusions can they draw about objects that are reflective?

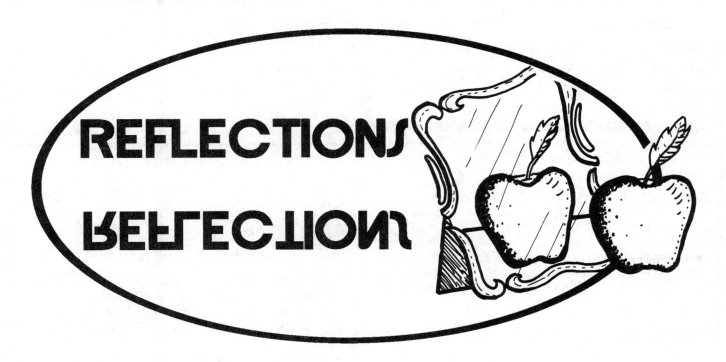

-- Cut and tape student directions inside kit. --

DIRECTIONS
Try this activity to show you how mirrors work to make a KALEIDOSCOPE.

1. Place a piece of white paper on the desk or table top. Put the triangle of three mirrors on the white paper.

2. Drop one piece of colored paper into the center of the triangular mirrors. How many pieces of paper do you see <u>reflected</u> in the mirrors?

3. Drop more pieces of colored paper into the center of the mirrors. Observe the pattern. This is how a kaleidoscope works.

4. Blow gently into the mirrors to move the bits of paper. Does the pattern in the mirrors change?

5. Remove the colored paper. Experiment with the button and penny in the center.

Inventory Checklist

❏ Replace the bits of colored paper in the bag. Clean the desk top completely.

❏ Use a tissue to wipe off any fingerprints you might have gotten on the mirrors.

❏ Be sure the button and penny are back in the kit.

Things to Think About

• What would happen if you taped more mirrors together?

• Why do people put a large mirror in a small room? How does it change the look of the room?

• Find out what a periscope is. Where is it used?

• How do automobile drivers use mirrors?

Hair-raising Fun!

Have you ever seen your hair stand on end—literally? Static electricity is the culprit!

TEACHING GUIDE
Preparation Notes

SKILLS

- observation
- drawing conclusions
- making hypotheses
- understanding positive/negative

PREPARATION

Background Information:
Everything around us, including our bodies, contains <u>electrons</u>, the smallest unit of electricity. Unlike charges—positive and negative—attract. When two objects rub against each other, one loses electrons and becomes positively charged. The other gains electrons and becomes negatively charged.

Materials:
8 squares of material *(substitute if necessary)*
- carpeting
- velvet
- felt
- satin
- wool
- knit
- burlap
- polyester
- styrofoam packing pieces

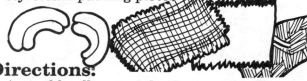

Directions:
1. Assemble all materials. Prepare the kit container and cover according to directions on page 5.
2. Store styrofoam pieces in a separate bag.

LITERATURE LINKS

Experiments with Static Electricity; *Harry Sootin.* The title says it all!

Exploring Electrostatics; *Raymond A. Wohlrabe.* Experiments with static electricity.

Dilly and the Horror Movie; *Tony Bradman.* The world's funniest—and naughtiest—dinosaur finds himself glued to the Late Show and some hair raising stories.

WRITING SPARKS

⬧ Read and write some "hair-raising" stories.

⬧ Discuss the terms *positive* and *negative*. Relate them to feelings and attitudes. Write two paragraphs for each:
  "Things that <u>affect</u> me positively."
  "Things that <u>affect</u> me negatively."
  "Things I <u>feel</u> positive about."
  "Things I <u>feel</u> negative about."

MORE TO EXPLORE

✔ Conduct another static electricity experiment. Provide students with an inflated balloon. Test static by rubbing the balloon against objects—including hair, skin and clothing. Observe interaction between the balloon and the object. Test for degree of electrical attraction between the balloon and the object by seeing if the balloon will stick to the wall.

✔ Take apart a flashlight or other items that are battery-operated. Examine the positive and negative ends of the batteries. Learn how to reassamble the batteries to make the right connection.

✔ Can you picture electricity? Try it in an art project:
- Make positive/negative pictures. (see illustration)
- Color bold lightning bolts. Wash with dark watercolor.
- Draw an underwater scene with electric eels. Find out about fishes that are electrically charged—(yes, that's true!).

Color, cut and laminate for kit cover.
See preparation instructions, page 5.

Reproduce Page for Use in Student Kit

Hair-raising Fun!

------- Cut and tape student directions inside kit. -------

DIRECTIONS

Static electricity can make your hair stand on end!
What else is affected by static electricity?

1. Take several styrofoam pieces out of the bag.

2. Rub a piece of styrofoam back and forth against one of the squares of material. You don't need to press very hard.

3. Now test the styrofoam to see how much electrical charge it got from the material.
  • Press the styrofoam to the wall. Does it stick?
  • Rub again and hold it near your skin. Does your hair stick up?

4. Test each piece of material the same way. Which seems to create the most static?

Inventory Checklist

☐ 8 squares of material
☐ styrofoam packing pieces.

• Count the squares and make sure you
  return 8 to the kit.

• Put all the styrofoam back in the bag and
  seal it tightly.

Things to Think About

• What else could you test for static electricity?
  Walk around the room and find other objects to
  rub with the styrofoam.

• Have you ever walked across the room and gotten
  a shock when you touched something? Or have
  you combed your hair and had it stick stright
  up? What do you think causes that to happen?
  What was the weather like on those days?

77

Soak It Up!

Students are sure to get absorbed, engrossed and totally involved in these absorption activities!

SKILLS

- observation
- drawing conclusions
- vocabulary development
- application

PREPARATION

Materials:

- waxed paper
- paper towel
- aluminum foil
- shallow plastic bowl or pie tin
- magnifying glass
- sandpaper
- felt
- sponge or foam rubber

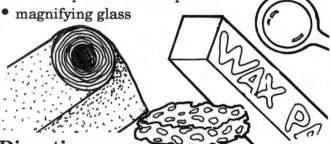

Directions:

1. Assemble all materials. Prepare the kit container and cover according to directions on page 5.
2. Cut each material into strips, 1" x 4" (2.54cm x 10 cm). These items (except for the sponge) are consumables. Cut 15 of each. Store in individual bags.

LITERATURE LINKS

Wonders of Sponges; *Morris Jacobson & Rosemary Pang.* The world of natural sponges and their capabilities.

Benjamin's 365 Birthdays; *Ron Barrett.* Nine-year old Benjamin gets absorbed by his birthday … and celebrates it all year long.

Mushroom in the Rain; *Mirra Ginsburg.* A group of creatures take shelter in the rain so they don't get soaked. A Russian tale.

WRITING SPARKS

- Discuss the different *meanings* of the word **absorbed**—engrossed, totally involved, — Describe something that totally absorbs you. It might be a baseball game, reading, playing dolls …

- Imagine that your body was able to absorb water. Describe what would happen when you swam, bathed or walked in the rain!

MORE TO EXPLORE

✔ Learn the meaning of absorption, the process by which substances gather up and evenly distribute matter or energy.

✔ Porous materials (those with holes) have greater absorbency qualities. Use magnifying glasses to look for materials that might be porous. Test your choices.

✔ Find out about other types of energy absorption—materials that absorb sound, colors that absorb heat or sustances, such as baking soda, that absorb smell.

✔ Take a walk after a rainstorm. How does nature absorb the water?

✔ What materials will absorb the most? Soak several items in water. Compare the results. Squeeze the absorbed water into measuring cups. Weigh the items before and after absorption. Test the ability of other liquids—milk, oil, soda—to be absorbed.

Soak It Up!

-- Cut and tape student directions inside kit. --

DIRECTIONS
Find out what absorbs—soaks up—the most water!

1. Take out one piece of material from each bag. There should be six (6). Check the inventory list to be sure you have them all. Pick up each material and feel it. Examine it in the magnifying glass. Predict which one you think will absorb the most water.

2. Fill the bowl or pie tin half way with water. Lay each material in the bowl so that one end is in the water. Look at the kit cover for help.

3. Watch each material carefully. Is it soaking up water? Use the magnifying glass to get a closer look. How can you tell if absorption is taking place? Keep track of how long it takes the items to absorb water. Do some absorb faster than others?

Inventory Checklist

- ❑ waxed paper
- ❑ paper towel
- ❑ aluminum foil
- ❑ shallow bowl or pie tin
- ❑ magnifying glass
- ❑ sandpaper
- ❑ sponge or foam rubber
- ❑ felt

• Throw away wet material except for the sponge. Squeeze the water out of the sponge and put it back in the bag. if any bags are

Things to Think About

• Which *absorbed* the most? the least? not at all?

• Did any of the materials look different through the magnifying glass? Do you see why one might be able to absorb more than another?

• Compare how each item **felt** before and **after** *absorption?* Would it weigh more or less?

A Little 💧 Will Do Ya'

TEACHING GUIDE
Preparation Notes

A drop of water can make a splash but can it make a hole? Kids will know the answer to this question after they've used the kit!

SKILLS

- observation
- measurement
- drawing conclusions
- comparing

PREPARATION

Materials:

- eye dropper
- paint stirrer
- 3 crayons — blue, red, green
- bottom half of a milk carton
- plastic cup
- box of toothpicks
- loose dirt

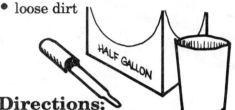

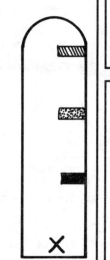

Directions:

1. Assemble all materials. Prepare the kit and cover according to directions on page 5.
2. Mark the paint stirrer with colored lines as shown.
3. Make a line with permanent marker on the milk carton, 2" (5cm) from the bottom.

LITERATURE LINKS

The Lampfish of Twill; *Janet Taylor Lisle.* A trip down a whirlpool to the ancient and beautiful core of the earth.

The King Who Rained; *Fred Gwynne.* Open those umbrellas—a cloudburst is dropping from his majesty.

Science Fun With Mud and Dirt; *Rose Wyler.* Reference for experiments and activities relating to the soil.

WRITING SPARKS

- Observe raindrops on a stormy day. Describe how the rain makes the earth look different. What would happen if the drops kept making bigger and bigger holes in the earth?

- **My Trip in a Drop of Water**

- What happens to a drop of water after it falls to earth? Make a diagram showing how water is processed.

MORE TO EXPLORE

✔ Conduct other experiments to measure the effect of an object's weight and the distance it is dropped on the size hole it makes. Try dropping a marble and ping pong ball on soil. Measure the depth of the hole created.

- Repeat the experiment. This time drop the marble and ping pong ball into water. Observe the depth both objects travel underwater when dropped from different heights. Make a picture report to show the results.

✔ Research some facts about craters.
- How is one formed?
- Where can they be found?
- Where is the largest one on earth? How big is it?

✔ Use plaster of Paris to make a model of a crater.

A Little Will Do Ya'

-------------------------------- Cut and tape student directions inside kit. --------------------------------

DIRECTIONS
Find out how deep a hole a drop of water can make.

1. Fill the milk carton with dirt up to the black line. Smooth out the dirt.

2. Put the X end of the paint stirrer against the edge of the carton, in the dirt.

3. Fill the cup with water. Take out three toothpicks and the crayons.

4. Fill the eye dropper with water and hold it over the dirt, even with the first blue line on the stick. Squeeze the dropper until a drop of water falls.

5. Measure the depth of the hole made by the drop. To so this, touch the end of one toothpick into the bottom of the hole. Make a blue mark at the place on the toothpick that is even with the top of the dirt. Color the toothpick blue from the mark to the tip that was in the hole.

6. Smooth out the dirt and repeat the experiment, this time dropping the water from the red line on the stick. Use a different toothpick. Repeat from the green line.

7. Line up the toothpicks, side by side. Compare the results.

Inventory Checklist

☐ eye dropper ☐ plastic cup
☐ paint stirrer ☐ toothpicks
☐ milk carton ☐ 3 crayons

• Take the paint stick out of the dirt and put the dirt back into the zip top bag. Seal it.
• Wipe out the milk carton and plastic cup.
• Throw away the toothpicks you used.

Things to Think About

• Why would the hole be deeper when the water was dropped from a higher level?

• How would the size of the hole change if you droped a marble instead of a drop of water?

• Would the results change if the soil were hard? What if the water was dropped into loose sand, or even water?

Let's Fly

Take a flight into history and science. on a paper airplane. Find out how airplanes work and how they changed the world.

SKILLS
- comparing
- application
- analysis
- research
- learning about transportation

PREPARATION

Materials:
- lightweight bond paper

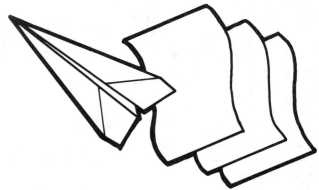

Directions:
1. Assemble all materials. Prepare the kit container and cover according to directions on page 5.
2. Make several folded paper airplane samples for the kit so that children can unfold and fold them prior to making their own. Mark them **SAMPLE.**

LITERATURE LINKS

First Flight; *McPhail.* A boy on his first plane trip is a model passenger, but his toy bear is a terror in the aisles.

Hello, This Is Your Penguin Speaking; *Rodney Rigby.* Penguin is the Wright brother of birds!

The Glorious FlightAcross the Channel with Louis Bleriot; *Alice and Martin Provenson.* Recreates the 1909 flight by this famous aviator.

WRITING SPARKS

∅ Have you ever been on an airplane trip? Tell about it. If you haven't, interview someone who has.

∅ Which form of transportation do you prefer… plane, boat, car or train? Why?

∅ If I could take a trip on a plane to anywhere in the world I would want it to take me to …

MORE TO EXPLORE

✔ Compare how long it would take to get to a destination using different modes of transportation. Discuss the pros and cons.

✔ Find out what jobs are available in aviation and travel. Invite a travel agent to visit class and share costs and flight times to destinations around the world. Ask a pilot to simulate a takeoff.

✔ Learn about famous **aviators.** •Write a report •Chart their flight on a map. • List their contributions to aviation.

✔ Have an airplane derbyflying student-designed paper planes. Which traveled the farthest, shortest, highest? Which did the most turns? Whick dove the quickest? Examine how each was built. What features made a plane fly better?

✔ Learn the art of **origami**—Japanese paper folding.

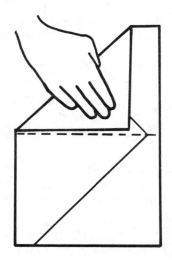

Color, cut and laminate for kit cover.
See preparation instructions, page 5.

Reproduce Page for Use in Student Kit

Let's Fly

-- Cut and tape student directions inside kit. --

DIRECTIONS

1. Study the paper airplane samples. Use a piece of paper from the kit and try to fold an airplane. Follow one of the patterns.

2. Try out your plane on a test flight. Be sure you check with your parent or a teacher for a safe place to fly your plane. Make several flights. Were the results the same each time?

3. Use one more piece of paper to fold a plane of your own design. Test this one too. Which plane flies better? Why?

Inventory Checklist

❑ airplane samples

❑ paper

• Add more paper if you used the last piece.

Things to Think About

• If airplanes are heavier than air, how can they fly? What keeps them up in the sky?

• How do the wings help a plane stay in the air?

• What's the difference between a glider and a jet?

• What changes have airplanes made in the world?

MAGNETIC FUN

The attraction to magnets is shared by young and old alike. Experiment with a variety of magnets and discover how much fun they can be.

SKILLS
- recording observations
- drawing conclusions
- working cooperatively
- counting

PREPARATION

Materials:
- several boxes of paper clips
- bar and horseshoe magnets in a variety of sizes and strengths
- Magnetic Fun Observation Record, page 86
- ziptop poly bag

Directions:
1. Assemble all materials. Prepare the kit container and cover according to directions on page 5. Note the number of each magnet on the student Inventory Checklist.
2. Store the paper clips in a ziptop poly bag.
3. Reproduce the Magnetic Fun observation record. These will be consumed by kit users so make approximately 15 copies.

LITERATURE LINKS

Exploring Magnets; *Ed Catherall.* Describes what magnets are and how they work—accompanying projects and activities.

Amazing Magnets; *David A. Adler.* An easy question-and-answer format provides basic information about magnets.

Experiments with Magnets; *Helen J. Challand.* An exciting collection of unusual experiments with magnets.

WRITING SPARKS

✎ List the different ways that magnets are used in business, school and around the home.

✎ Describe someone with a "magnetic personality."

✎ Write about the time you were picked up by a giant magnet. Where did it take you? Describe your adventure.

MORE TO EXPLORE

✔ Test a variety of substances (metal, plastic, etc.) for their magnetic quality. Make a chart showing the results.

✔ Bring the largest magnet you can find to class. Measure the farthest distance at which it can attract.

✔ Build a "Magnetic Sculpture" using a variety of magnets and items with magnetic qualities. How high can it be built? Take it apart and create a different sculpture.

✔ Turn a filing cabinet into a display for a class magnet collection. Share the origin of the magnet.

Color, cut and laminate for kit cover.
See preparation instructions, page 5.

MAGNETIC FUN

----------------------------------- Cut and tape student directions inside kit. -----------------------------------

DIRECTIONS

1. Spread the paper clips on a desk or table top. Experiment
with a variety of magnets to see how many clips you can pick
up with each one. Change the part of the magnet you are
placing against the paper clips and observe any differences
in the results.

2. Count the number of paper clips picked up by each magnet.
Record the results on the *Magnetic Fun Observation Record*
that is in the kit.

3. Repeat the experiment. Are the numbers about the same
when you count the second time?

Inventory Checklist

• This kit contains _____ bar magnets and
_____ horseshoe magnets. Please be sure
all magnets are returned to the kit.

• Check the floor for any paper clips that
may have fallen. Return all paper clips to
the ziptop bag and seal it.

Things to Think About

• What kind of magnets are generally stronger?
Why do you think that is the case?

• What toys do you have that use magnets?

• What happens when two magnets are placed
near each other?

Use with **MAGNETIC FUN**, pages 84-85.
Reproduce and cut into fourths.

Magnetic Fun
Observation Record

BAR
small medium large

end

middle

HORSESHOE
small medium large

end

middle

Magnetic Fun
Observation Record

BAR
small medium large

end

middle

HORSESHOE
small medium large

end

middle

Magnetic Fun
Observation Record

BAR
small medium large

end

middle

HORSESHOE
small medium large

end

middle

Magnetic Fun
Observation Record

BAR
small medium large

end

middle

HORSESHOE
small medium large

end

middle

Name_____ | Name_____ | Name_____

Date ——————————— | Date ——————————— | Date ———————————

Time Temperature Recorded: | Time Temperature Recorded: | Time Temperature Recorded:

———————————— | ———————————— | ————————————

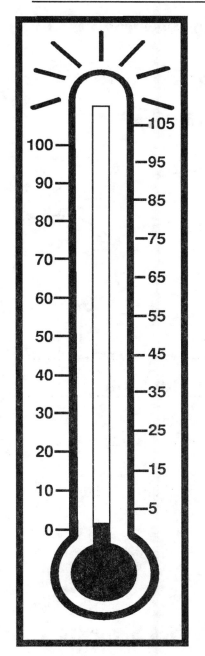 | 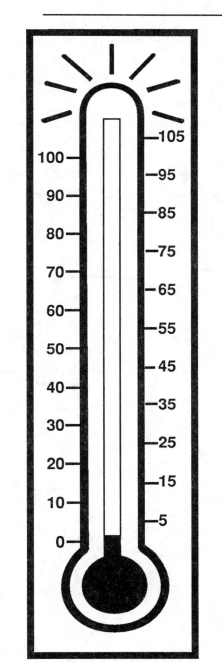 |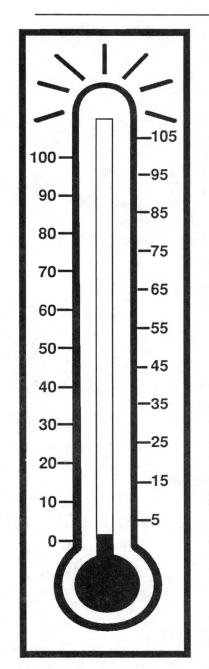

TODAY'S WEATHER: | TODAY'S WEATHER: | TODAY'S WEATHER:

rain_____ windy _____ | rain_____ windy _____ | rain_____ windy _____

snow_____ sunny _____ | snow_____ sunny _____ | snow_____ sunny _____

cloudy_____ humid _____ | cloudy_____ humid _____ | cloudy_____ humid _____

other_____ | other_____ | other_____

————————————— | ————————————— | —————————————

Use with **STAR GAZERS**, pages 68-69.

Aries the Ram
Draco the Dragon
Cancer the Crab
Perseus
Great Dog
(Canis Major)
Leo the Lion
Taurus the Bull
Hydra the Sea Serpent

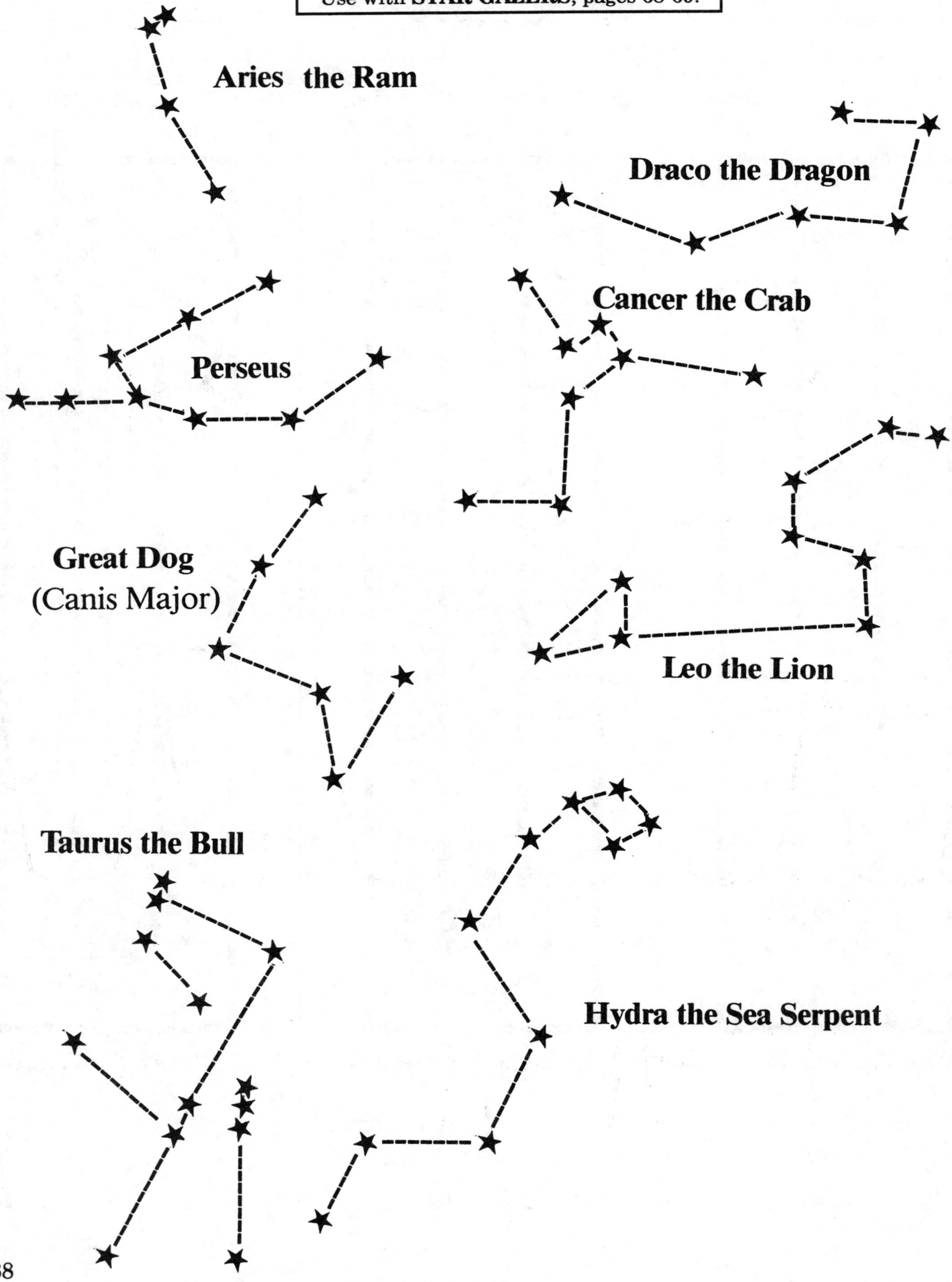

Use with **GET IT IN GEAR**, pages 56-57.

Use with **ALL MIXED UP,** pages 48-49

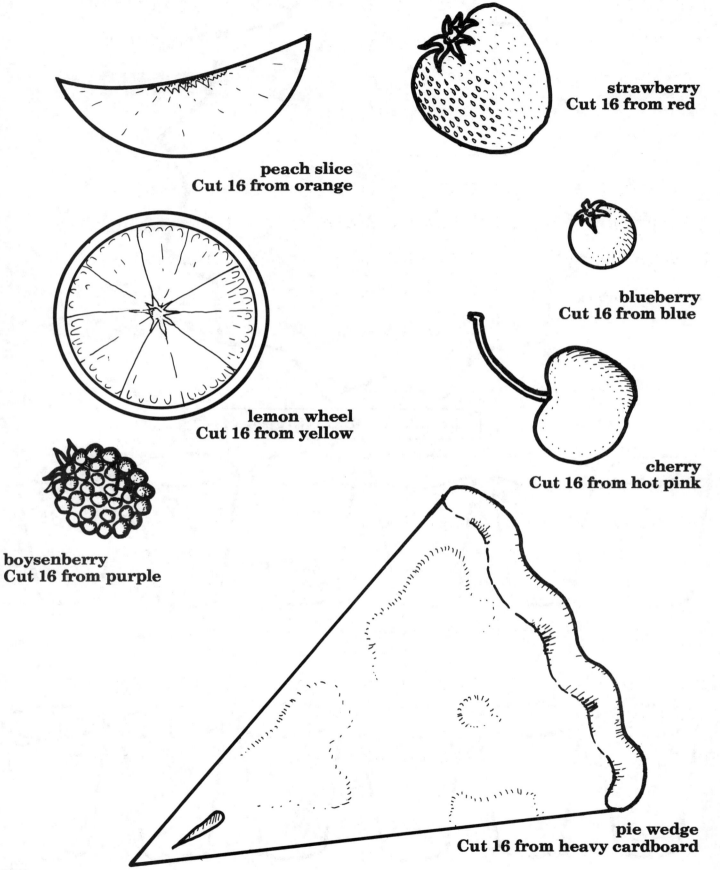

peach slice
Cut 16 from orange

strawberry
Cut 16 from red

lemon wheel
Cut 16 from yellow

blueberry
Cut 16 from blue

cherry
Cut 16 from hot pink

boysenberry
Cut 16 from purple

pie wedge
Cut 16 from heavy cardboard

Party of 2

1/2 want strawberry

1/2 want cherry

Party of 6

1/3 want boysenberry

1/3 want lemon

1/3 want blueberry

Party of 4

1/4 want peach

3/4 want strawberry

Party of 5

2/5 want blueberry

1/5 want cherry

2/5 want peach

Party of 8

1/2 want strawberry

2/8 want lemon

2/8 want blueberry

3/8 want cherry

Party of 6

1/2 want blueberry

1/3 want cherry

1/6 want peach

Party of 3

2/3 want boysenberry

1/3 want blueberry

Party of 4

1/2 want lemon

1/2 want peach

Party of 6

1/2 want strawberry

1/3 want lemon

1/3 want blueberry

1/3 want cherry

Party of 9

1/3 want peach

1/3 want lemon

2/3 want strawberry

1/3 want blueberry

Party of 6

2/6 want strawberry

2/6 wanat boysenberry

1/6 want cherry

1/6 want lemon

Party of 8

1/4 want blueberry

1/2 want cherry

1/4 want peach

Use with **PIZZA PARTY,** pages 18-19.

pepperoni

mushroom

olive

**green
pepper**

cheese

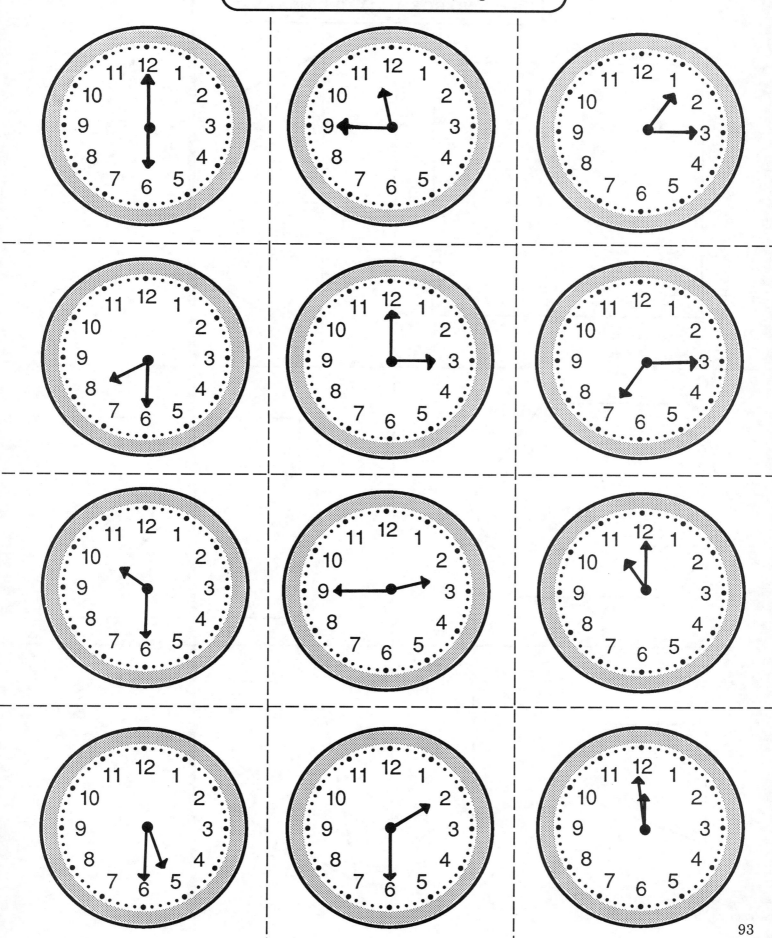

Use with **NO-BORE BOARDS**, pages 8-9.

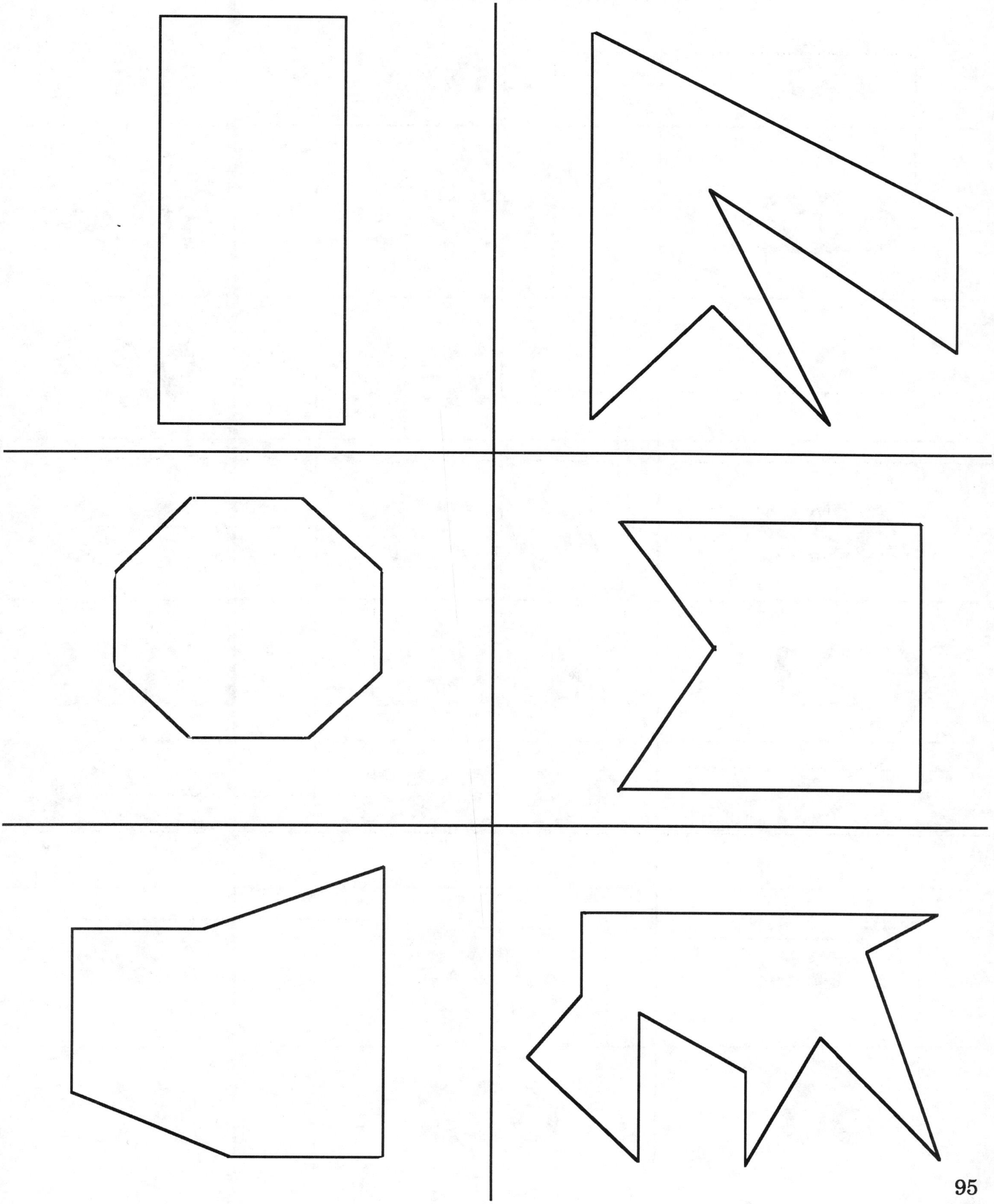

23	36	44
622	307	526
9	152	93
622	4,476	2,105
6,271	4,092	1,353
21,462	16,395	12,400
768	593	486
66	632	94